Ray Barron-Woolford is a life-time community activist, broadcaster, playright, and author. His most recent play is *Liberty* about Kath Duncan's role in establishing the LGBTQ and civil rights movement in 1930's Britain, laying the groundwork for The National Council Civil Liberties.

Reviews

Many women have been written out of the male-dominated history books. For every Amazonian queen, rebel girl, scandalous mistress, militant suffragette or persistent female pioneer that we now know about, there are hundreds more "hidden her stories" of extraordinary women which go totally uncelebrated.

Ray Woolford's fascinating new book shines the spotlight on an unsung political heroine whom many will be unfamiliar with. Kath Duncan was one of the most important activists of the last century. She had connections with major politicians like Winston Churchill and George Lansbury, she stood for Parliament, made inspiring speeches and dedicated her entire life to the causes she believed in to the detriment of her own health. However, her leading role in left-wing and communist politics, her working class Scottish background and her gender, have all led to her story being marginalized. Her important contribution to the civil rights movement has been buried by the establishment since her death in 1954, at the height of the Cold War.

Woolford's book tells how Kath Duncan was a highly significant champion of the poor and the unemployed. She was a tireless campaigner for workers' rights and spent two jail terms in Holloway prison for making political speeches. The National Council for Civil Liberties supported her in a landmark court case on the freedom of speech but not many history books will tell you that fact. Duncan also opposed Fascism, took part in the Battle of Cable Street and was central to the Aid to Spain movement in the 1930s. She was a key player in these things – so by rights she should be a household name or have a memorial or statue erected somewhere.

Woolford's very well researched biography defiantly places Kath Duncan's story right back into the public eye where it belongs, and restores her to her rightful position as one of the leading civil-rights activists of our time. Her political campaigning can be linked to several of the most significant moments in 20th century British history and has relevance to many of the social and political issues we have today.

In a year when we are celebrating 100 years of some women getting the vote in the UK – it is vital that we also recognise and acknowledge the life and work of Kath Duncan – a working class woman who played just as significant a role in politics as the Pankhursts, Nancy Astor or Barbara Castle. In a world where we constantly strive for more equality this book has an important message about how society deals with freedom of speech and civil liberty. Kath Duncan's story has finally been uncovered by Woolford and all of us really ought to read it.

Chrissy Hamlin (www.chrissyhamlin.blogspot.co.uk)
The Hidden Herstories Blog and #WomensHistoryHour on twitter

The Last Queen of Scotland is a veritable banquet of forgotten history mixed with Woolford's own love story for one of the greatest women most people have never heard of. Immediately accessible, the author has crafted an important and pertinent public record of a figure who encapsulates so many of today's struggles. The banishing of the mists of time from Kath Duncan's life could well stand as one of Woolford's finest achievements.

Steve Topple, activist, broadcaster, political commentator and
writer for The Canary

I must be honest, I had heard very little about Kath until Ray introduced me to her, and I'm so thankful that he did. He takes you on the journey of Kath's life, starting from her childhood and later her friendships with several people including Churchill.
Ray describes everything with such clarity and precision which made me feel like I know Kath and that I can certainly relate to her.

I was shocked to have found that the little that I had previously read about Kath was inaccurate and Ray has gone to great lengths to correct this, and quite rightly so.
Kath was a truly amazing woman, fierce but kind, fair and understanding. She is an inspiration to all women worldwide.

I give this book a 5-star rating because it doesn't get better than this and I fully recommend this book to people of all ages.

Thank you, Ray.

Charlotte Hughes writes for The Morning Star and The Guardian and writes a very high profile blog The Poor Side of Life

There is no doubt that the most important period for ordinary people in Scotland and England was between the Wars especially after the Russian Revolution, the First World War and the start of the Second and whilst today many commentators talk about the similarities from the 1930s to the present age of Trump and the rise of Fascism again across Europe the 1930s is an era we should all be reading up on.

This extraordinary, extensively researched book puts at its core the true story of Kath Duncan who was very different from the other Scot from Kirkcaldy who is still celebrated across the globe today, the economist Adam Smith. Kath Duncan was probably the most important Scottish and UK civil rights activist over the past 100 years, whose imprisonment laid the ground work for The National Council of Civil Liberties (which these days is called Liberty), which is also the title of another must-read book about Kath Duncan who, until this book, you probably knew nothing about.

Kath Duncan – leader, suffragette, LGBT, civil rights campaigner, leader of Hunger Marches, anti-war, anti-fascist, activist against the Spanish Civil War, supporter of Gandhi and Indian workers for union recognition, as well as taking on the utility companies, the King, Parliament and the entire legal system.

Kath Duncan may have been so small she needed a soap box to become her stage, but her glamour, courage and inspiration for many in 30s Britain led many to call her the people's Queen.

In the year we celebrate 100 years of Women's activism is it not time we bring Kath Duncan out of the shadows and let her shine with the stars?

This book screams period drama. Make me a movie, but most of all raises one crucial question we should all be asking, especially those in education and in the position to make statues and put up plaques. Why do we celebrate Kings, Queens, tyrants and the children of the elite who became activists, but selectively erase working class heroes especially women like Kath Duncan whose activism won us all the freedoms we all enjoy today?

You don't have to love history or politics to enjoy this book. The Last Queen of Scotland takes you on a ride through the world in the 1930s, through the life of Kath and puts the case why she is the most important Scot and UK civil rights activist in the past 100 years from Kirkcaldy to Hackney to Deptford and back.
I rate this book 5 stars; everyone should read this book and ensure she becomes the household name she deserves to be!

Who will be first to erect a Statue to remember and give thanks to such a great activist of inspiration and courage – Kirkcaldy, Scotland, London, Hackney, Camden, Deptford, and Lewisham?

The London Economic

This book is dedicated to working-class heroes, especially women like Kath Duncan who were, for far too long, left in the shadow of history. I hope through this work to bring them out of the shadows to walk with the stars.

Ray Barron-Woolford

THE LAST QUEEN
OF SCOTLAND

AUSTIN MACAULEY PUBLISHERS™

London • Cambridge • New York • Sharjah

Ordering Information:
Quantity sales: special discounts are available on quantity purchases by corporations, associations, and others. For details, contact the publisher at the address below.

Publisher's Cataloging-in-Publication data
Barron-Woolford, Ray
The Last Queen of Scotland

ISBN 9781643782690 (Paperback)
ISBN 9781643782706 (Hardback)
ISBN 9781643782713 (Kindle e-book)
ISBN 9781645363576 (ePub e-book)

Library of Congress Control Number: 2019935776

The main category of the book — History / Europe / Great Britain / Scotland

www.austinmacauley.com/us

First Published (2019)
Austin Macauley Publishers LLC
40 Wall Street, 28th Floor
New York, NY 10005
USA

mail-usa@austinmacauley.com
+1 (646) 5125767

Table of Contents

Introduction

In 1966, it was decided that a large social housing development should be built on the banks of the River Thames, in Deptford. This huge, state-of-the-art housing estate, which included some of the highest tower blocks in the country, would become the Pepys estate, named after Samuel Pepys, the famous diarist. One of the tower blocks was named Daubeney Tower, after the 1st baron, Daubeney, and it is extraordinary that the council did not see the irony in this choice of name for a block of homes intended to house the poorest in the city.

Lord Daubeney commanded King Henry VII's army during the Cornish Rebellion of 1497. He was captured by the peasants' army of Michael Joseph (An Gof) but subsequently released, unharmed, by his captors as a sign of goodwill. Daubeney did not return the favor. After the battle of Deptford Bridge, in which the peasants' army was defeated, Daubeney went on to slaughter the leaders of the rebellion and their poor followers in their thousands.

There is some irony, then, in the fact that, in 1966, the local authority chose to celebrate the life of this man, who was anything but a friend of the poor, especially those who demanded social justice, by naming after him social dwellings designed to accommodate such people in a comfortable and dignified way. It would have been much more appropriate to have named the building Audley Tower, after the 7th baron, Audley, a knight of the realm who recognized the justice of the peasants' cause and fought shoulder-to-shoulder with the leaders of the Cornish Rebellion at the battle of Deptford Bridge. He has been all but erased from history, unlike other leaders and champions of the poor at the time, such as Jack Cade (1450), Wat Tyler (1381), Michael Joseph (An Gof, 1497), and Sir Tomas Wyatt (1554), all of whom played a hugely important role in Deptford's largely forgotten working-class history, just like the subject of this book, Kath Duncan.

What is it that sees to the fact that our cultural and educational establishments allow us to celebrate the lives of our kings and queens, and even tyrants, while it seems to take positive and deliberate steps to eradicate the memory and legacy of the heroes of the working-class' struggle, especially women like Kath Duncan? What kind of mindset could think that a housing development should be used to perpetuate the name of a man who despised the peasants and the poor, and who relished killing so many of them, rather than that of anyone from a staggeringly wide array of real heroes and champions of the ordinary working-class people, throughout the centuries, who came to the shores of Deptford, one of the nation's greatest centers of workers' heritage? This area, from which 500 working families set sail with Peter the Great to build the first Russian navy, played an important role in building the nation's wealth through trade and industry made possible by the blood and sweat of the working people, including slaves, whose labor shaped not just Deptford but the world.

When I started the We Care Foodbank in Deptford, several years ago, I never expected that it would become the nation's largest foodbank, which paid its staff a wage, bought most of the food and toiletries that were distributed every day, opened six days a week, and maintained a crucial lifeline for thousands of people. It was in 2015 that I organized a local heritage festival to raise funds for our work, and it was while I was working on a book about Deptford's remarkable history and heritage that I first came across Kath Duncan.

My first book, *Deptford*, contained my first brief presentation of the life, work, and importance of this remarkable woman. And then, after writing Food Bank Britain, I wrote the play *Liberty* about just one chapter in the amazing life of this remarkable woman who was so much more than your usual troublemaking activist.

Since the day I first became aware of her, she has haunted my mind and my thoughts almost constantly, day and night, and I wanted to learn as much about her as I could. Now, after four years' research, I present what I have discovered in this book. And, I hope that as you read through these pages – which reveal something of her amazing but, in many ways, tragic life – you will come to agree with me that Kath Duncan was the most important civil rights activist in the UK of the past 100 years. No other woman was so effective at such a high level in taking direct action against social injustice and inequality, poor housing, fuel poverty, the arms trade, fascism in all its forms, and discrimination against women and LGBT people, all the while demanding and working tirelessly to try and achieve social justice and full civil rights for all.

If nothing else, I hope this book leads to a wider debate on the issue of whose work and legacy achieves cultural recognition and how we can find and choose our own heroes in a time of great cultural change, in which social media plays such an important role, and growing public disillusionment with the nation's governing elite.

Do we celebrate them with a plaque, a street name, a festival, or a special day? How do we celebrate these troublesome, often difficult, but precious heroes who, like Kath, would always tell others: 'Fight to the last ditch!' As they did themselves. I sincerely hope that the story of *The Last Queen of Scotland* will do something to ensure that Kath Duncan will no longer be left in the shadows but will be honored as one of our nation's greats.

Repeated police charge in Royal Mint Street, attempting to clear the street for the Fascist parade

SPECIAL THANKS

Special thanks:
- Doctor and playwright Tom Band, Karen Makins.
- George Stevenson, whose first article on Kath Duncan sent me on this journey.
- Scottish historians Prof John Foster, Ian MacDougall, David Potter, and George Proudfoot.
- The inspirational Oonagh Stanley Toffolo

Book references:
- *Deptford, A Radical History* – Ray Barron-Woolford
- *Liberty*, the play-book of the struggle for civil rights and Kath Duncan's fight to establish National Council civil liberties – Ray Barron-Woolford
- *Kirkcaldy Parliamentarians* – Dave Potter
- *What Price Liberty* – Ben Wilson
- *The Tragedy of European Labour, 1918–1939* – Adolf Sturmthal
- *History of Communist Party of Great Britain 1927–1941* – Noreen Branson
- *Communists & British Society, 1920–1991* – K. Morgan, G. Cohen, and A. Flinns
- *The Voice of Silence* – Oonagh Stanley Toffolo
- *Reason in Revolt* – Fred Copeman
- *Lions Led by Jackals, Stalinism in the International Brigades* – Dale Street
- *The Hunger Marches in Britain, 1920–1940* – Peter Kingsford

Archives used for reference:
- Lewisham Studies & Archive
- Greenwich Heritage Centre
- Marx Memorial Library & Workers School
- Alan Smith Institute
- Brighton and Hove Archive
- Modern Records Centre, Warwick University
- Fife Archives
- Kirkcaldy Library, Archive, and Museum
- Kirkcaldy Historical Society
- Hackney Archive
- Camden Archive at Holborn Library
- The British Library
- The National Archive
- The Churchill Archive
- Communist Party Archive
- City of London Archive
- Wandsworth Heritage Centre
- House of Commons Archive

- National Records of Scotland
- Home Office
- Working Class Movement Library – Salford
- Peoples History Huseum – Salford
- London Metropolitan Museum
- Glasgow City Archive
- University of Warwick
- Glasgow Life
- Glasgow Family History

Newspaper archive credits:
- *The South London Press*
- *The Fife Free Press*
- *The Kentish Mercury*
- *The Daily worker*
- *The Birmingham Evening Mail*
- *The Times*
- *The Express*
- *The Daily Telegraph*

A Strong Woman vs. A Woman of Strength

A strong woman works every day to keep her body in shape...
But a woman of strength builds relationships to keep her soul in shape.
A strong woman isn't afraid of anything.
But, a woman of strength shows courage in the midst of fear
A strong woman won't let anyone get the better of her.
But, the woman of strength gives the best of herself to everyone.
A strong woman makes mistakes and avoids the same ones in the future.
A woman of strength realizes that life's mistakes can also be unexpected blessings and capitalizes on them.
A strong woman has faith that she is strong enough for the journey.
But, the woman of strength has faith that it is in the journey that she will become strong.

Martha S. Hardy

Chapter 1
Winston Churchill's Apprentice

With a classroom of children to teach, a never-ending queue of people needing her help to both read and write letters in the middle of a war, and plays to perform at her amateur dramatics group, Kath could be forgiven for having one of those full-on busy days which we have all had. Such days when we find we have put on odd socks, or our top inside out, or, in Kath's case, rushing from performing on stage to a meeting with the ever-busy and dashing Winston Churchill... and forgetting to remove her stage makeup.

"Well, it's not every parliamentary candidate who gets the endorsement and office help of Mary, Queen of Scots," Churchill said to the beautiful but strange-looking woman sitting in wait for him.

Somewhat annoyed with herself at having been so busy on this most important of occasions that she had overlooked the makeup, pointing her gloved hands to her face, covered in makeup for her next performance in an hour's time, Kath said, "Am I not Elizabeth I?"

Winston roared with laughter: "Yes, Kath, and I cannot think of a better person to organize and win my campaign."

Churchill was under pressure to get a strong election campaign team in place if he was to secure his seat in parliament as the new MP for Dundee, in 1917. Just two years earlier, he had been demoted from his role as First Lord of the Admiralty; this was after the huge loss of life in the Gallipoli and Dardanelles naval campaigns, for which he was responsible. He resigned from government, and in 1916, became a capable army officer on the frontline.

In 1917, Prime Minister David Lloyd George wanted Winston Churchill to become the new minister for munitions.

Therefore, the then MP for Dundee traded his seat in the House of Commons for a seat in the House of Lords to give Winston Churchill the chance of once again sitting on government benches in the House of Commons. His wife, Clementine, had found him the perfect candidate to run his campaign team and to mobilize the workers in his support: her friend, Kath MacColl.

Kath was born on 4th July, 1888, in the rural Scottish village of Tarbert. She was named after her father's mother, Catherine Sinclair, whilst her sister would be named after her mother's mother. In 1893, when Kath was just 5-years-old, her father, Archibald MacColl, a merchant, died at just 39-years-old and the family moved to 9 Sterling Cottage, Kirkden, in Argyllshire. This was to be close to her grandparents on her mother's side, George and Margaret Stephens.

These children marched in a South Wales demonstration against the means test and welfare reform

The loss of her father and the man of the house must have had a traumatic impact on Kath, her sister Margaret, and her mother, Agnes Gibson Stevens.

Agnes, who had been born in Kirkden Parish, in Angus, on 3rd July, 1860, was known as 'Mama' to everyone. In the difficult period after the loss of her husband, her Christian faith kept her going and her sewing and dress-making skills provided the family with a basic income, skills which would later ensure that Kath wore the latest handmade designs that would allow her to impress at the highest levels of society. The local community also rallied to the family's aid, making sure that they did not end up in the workhouse. Kath's sister, Margaret, grew up to marry John McCowan and have two children, Elspeth Margaret McGowan and Ada Stewart McCowan. Although Kath had no children of her own, Margaret's daughter, Elspeth, made up for it. She had four children with her husband, Robert Maurice Jacobi, three girls – Lorne, Sally, and Barbara – and a son, Clive.

Kath's family roots were as radical as she would become. Although Margaret would take a less political path, they were both proud of the fact their great-grandmother was a descendant of the Scottish folk hero Rob Roy, who was said never to have 'lifted' a poor man's beast. In his youth, Kath's great-grandfather had gallantly taken the place of an older, married man who had been seized by the press-gang. And on returning from the wars, he ran off with the daughter of his master. Her grandfather had been a man well respected for feeding the hungry during the 'years of the short corn'.

Kath attended the village school in Kirkden and worked hard, securing a scholarship to high school and another scholarship to St. Andrews University, Dundee, where she studied literature. In between helping local people write letters to their loved ones on the Western front and giving comfort to the far too many getting terrible news, Kath started to become active in the Independent Labour Party and the Suffragette movement.

Kath became friends with Churchill's wife, Clementine, when she lived for a period in Edinburgh while attending the Karl Frobel School. Clementine Churchill, like Kath, had a strong sense of social justice, and the two had a close bond from the moment they met, although they clearly came from very different backgrounds. Clementine's family had moved to Scotland from Dieppe, in France, after Clementine's elder sister, Kitty, had contracted the tuberculosis that would take her life on 5 March, 1900. The same disease would also take Kath's life.

Kath's School in Kirkcaldy

Churchill would grade women he liked according to two criteria: they must have 'beauty' and 'distinction', and Kath had both, and more.

It was impossible not to be struck by Kath MacColl's appearance: she was always immaculately dressed in the latest style, wearing gloves, and with a hat to set off her beautiful red hair and blue eyes to their best effect.

Clementine Churchill had pleaded with Kath, as a friend, to help her husband win the Dundee seat and fight off a very real challenge from Tories. Kath readily agreed, as she always did whenever she was asked to help, and found herself flying hectically between her amateur stage performances and Churchill's tight schedule.

At the time, Kath lived in rooms at 92 High Street, Kirkcaldy. She had secured a job as a teacher at the East School, a primary school in Kirkcaldy (now the Glebe Park Neighbourhood Centre).

During the Great War, it was her job to teach girls who spent most of their day working in the factories and mills. Despite their exhaustion, the children had huge affection for Kath and a real eagerness to learn from her, which in turn, made her task very satisfying and rewarding. After the war, her classes consisted of unemployed girls whom she would teach and inspire in exactly the same way. But, this was not enough to satisfy Kath's need and desire to do what she could in the fight to defend and support the 'underprivileged'. Kath was always to be found assisting at food kitchens, helping the sick, and teaching everyone and anyone how to read and write.

Kath was precise, well-organized, and smart, with a huge love of books and a massive hunger to learn. Living on the 'Lang Toun' – Kirkcaldy's 6.4-kilometre-long high street – and close to the bustling docks, an important center for the trade in coal, salt, linen, and linoleum – just like Adam Smith, 2 centuries previously – gave Kath a real insight into the economic dynamics of the world and shaped her perspective on the political, social, and economic problems of the age and their solutions. Although, her views and those of the author of *The Wealth of Nations* could not have been more different.

Kath's friendship with the Churchills, which gave her access to people from the highest levels of society and the country's most interesting and controversial radicals and suffragettes, also gave her a distinctive insight into the world and the war. Billed as the war that would end all wars, the devastation was immense. It must have been almost impossible for Kath to comprehend what Winston Churchill, who was on the frontline in 1916, would report of the war and the staggering loss of life.

By the end of WWI, it would be estimated that 37 million people had died as a direct consequence of the war. 6 million died of disease and starvation. 250,000 British Tommies would come home with partial or full amputations, only to have to eke out a living begging on the nation's streets, while 908,000 British men never came home.

Kath was particularly alarmed at the way in which all the men from one village were put together as one fighting unit, which ensured that they fought together but also died together. This meant that all the menfolk from entire families and villages could be wiped out together. Russia, a country for whose history Kath shared a love for with Clementine, lost 1.7 million people, whilst having to care for a staggering 4.9 million people, taking the greatest share of the pain. It would be

Kath's influence that would lead to Clementine Churchill becoming an active member of Friends of Russia.

However odd it must have seemed to those around Winston Churchill, Kath had become a firm friend at a time when people of her class would not usually be permitted through the front door and certainly would not be recognized as a friend. Yet, in 1908, Kath was at the Churchills' wedding in London with many of the most significant people of the time. Clementine Churchill introduced Kath to the leading members of the Suffragette movement, while Kath would introduce her to Willie Gallacher. This was the man who, in 1935, would be the United Kingdom's first elected communist MP for West Fife, a seat he would hold until 1950, when he would lose it to The Labour Party.

These three distinctive and determined individuals felt the same about the Tories, whom Clementine described as 'vulgar'. How she felt when her own Winston joined the Conservative Party is not known. And although Kath received support from the suffragette activists, she felt that none of the women truly understood the real crises facing the nation: poverty, inequality, social injustice, and an absence of meaningful civil rights. How could it be right and just that working women did not have the vote, while their labor, often in truly appalling conditions, made others hugely rich, all while their menfolk were being sent to fight and die in the country's wars? How could it be right and just that children were freezing to death in slum housing conditions without adequate nutrition or health care?

***

This, then, was the situation in 1917. And as Kath's friend Clementine found a new, active role working for the Young Men's Christian Association (YMCA) in setting up canteens for munitions workers across the North East, Kath found herself in the new role of Winston Churchill's apprentice, helping him fight an election campaign and learning the art of politics. Churchill himself spent very little time campaigning and left much of the election strategy and the mobilizing of the popular vote to Kath, whose street activism at the gates of factories and pits secured him the seat. This he won on 6 May with a staggering 80% of the vote. 1917 was also the year in which her beloved sister and fellow teacher, Margaret, married, on 20 July, in the United Free Church of Scotland, in Kirkcaldy.

Kath's lodgings in Kirkcaldy

Kath's involvement in this political campaign and her association with the Churchills very much represents her political coming of age.

But, this campaign also brought her closer to her fellow teacher and activist, Sandy (Alexander) Duncan. The son of a railway goods supervisor, Sandy also taught at the East School in Kirkcaldy, and his inspirational teaching of sport to the children was greatly admired and respected by his colleagues. With his rugged good looks, he was a perfect match for the striking and stylish Kath, who was already regarded as one of the great beauties of the age. And even though married teachers were simply not allowed, they were married on 23 December, 1923, at the Carlton Tea Rooms in Kirkcaldy, just as his parents, David and Mary, had done on 30 December, 1892.

What I find particularly interesting about the marriage of the popular Kath and Sandy Duncan is the fact that only the minimum number of people attended the wedding ceremony.

Only two people were present to witness the marriage, and it is striking that neither Kath's mother nor her sister Margaret were there. Kath's mother was devoted to her daughter and lived with and supported her until her death. She was also deeply religious and, although this would not have necessarily prevented her attending Kath and Sandy's civil ceremony, it has led me to think there might have been something else about this marriage that kept her away. Given the libertarian nature of the Duncan household, particularly in London, and especially its openness to and support of the persecuted and marginalized, including transvestites and gay people, it has occurred to me that the Duncans' marriage may have been a marriage of convenience between two people of gay or non-polar sexuality which would have protected them and enabled them to engage in their very public activism without the nature of their own private lives becoming a distraction.

Although in 1922 Churchill lost the seat that he, and Kath, had won so convincingly, Kath had served her apprenticeship, gaining valuable contacts and an insight at the highest level into how politics worked and how powerful men operated. She was a strong woman who knew she had the ability and strength to take on the world and its injustices, and with her handsome and loyal Sandy at her side, that is exactly what she did.

In January, 1924, Kath followed her beloved Sandy to his home at 49 Downs Road Clapton, in Hackney, London. Here, she would be involved with other passions in her life: Hackney Dramatics Society, the PLEBs, Sylvia Pankhurst, the Cohen sisters, and a life of activism.

Kath Duncan addressing 30,000 people at the Gasworks
Protest, 1936

It is very probable that both Kath and Sandy were LGBTQ, but as it was illegal at the time, they chose to get married as a way of disguising their sexuality. This book, I hope, helps you draw your own conclusions

Unity Is Their Slogan

UNITY IS STRENGTH

WAKE UP, THE WICK. WE HAVE HAD AGONY WICK LONG ENOUGH

INGRAMS RECORD 1931 for Workers 5% WAGE CUT

INGRAMS RECORD 1933 to Share-Holders

Striking rubber workers at the conclusion of their dinner-hour demonstration yesterday.

Rubber workers at the conclusion of their dinner-hour demonstration

Chapter 2
Love and a New Life in London

In January, 1924, Kath followed her beloved Sandy to the new home he had already established in London, at 49 Downs Road, adjoining Hackney Downs Park, E5. And, her arrival was greeted with much excitement by Hackney's extensive network of activists. After her record of community activism, her support for the suffragette movement, her extensive social network – in large part due to her friendship with Clementine Churchill – and her success in the Dundee by-election, who would not want to meet and work with this dashing, engaging woman? Kath and Sandy had it all: good looks, humor, style, and the skills to mobilize thousands and the hopes of the community to secure the revolution they all craved.

Kath was the toast of the radical left. Many shared her support of the Russian Revolution, even Clementine Churchill, who, through Kath's influence, had a love of all things Russian. She became the chair of the Red Cross Aid to Russia fund during World War One, and while on a tour of Russia, towards the end of World War II, she was awarded the Order of the Red Banner of Labour by the Russian government, on behalf of the nation.

Although interest in Lenin's revolution was widespread, the Communist Party only officially established itself in Britain in 1920. And many suffragettes, like Kath, transferred their allegiance from the women's movement to communism.

Kath had never been a single-issue activist, and her increasing political activism and awareness made her very unhappy with the limited extension of the franchise brought about by the Representation of the People Act, 1918. Although all men over 21-years-old were given the franchise in this act, it seemed to Kath that this was the very least the state could do after so many Tommies lost their lives in the war. And she was far from happy that only propertied women would secure the vote. For Kath, the working class consisted of women, men, and children of all faiths, color, and genders; and real activism had to be about a social justice agenda that ended the class system, along with the gross inequality and crushing poverty it produced.

In the post-war context, Kath would stand out from the crowd and become arguably the greatest UK civil rights activist of the past 100 years; no other activist was as forceful as her in her leadership in so many different campaigns centered around her clear civil rights and social justice agenda. Kath would join and work her hardest for any and every group that shared her values and was tireless and amazingly effective in mobilizing others to fight and put an end to so much injustice.

Although Kath found a teaching post at The Battersea Continuation School, in South London, where she continued to help and inspire the children as she had in Scotland, Hackney seemed the best place to live. Kath was always careful to maintain a clear distance between her work as a teacher and her life outside the school as a political activist.

Before they had been married, Sandy had already secured the post of sports master at a school in Bermondsey, a job he excelled at; he ensured that the school's trophy cabinet was always filled with tokens of success of the school's sports clubs under his inspired leadership.

GALLACHER IN

Election Result
In West Fife

COMMUNIST WINS
MINING SEAT

" Victory For Working-Class
Unity Against National Govt."

GREAT HELP FROM U.M.S.

WILLIAM GALLACHER, Communist, made history yesterday when he was elected Member of Parliament for West Fife by a Majority of 593 votes.

The votes were: Gallacher, 13,462. Adamson (Labour), 12,869, Milne (Conservative), 9,667.

This splendid victory was received with scenes of tremendous enthusiasm in Fife, which a couple of hours later was spreading among workers throughout the country and especially in the Rhondda where the valleys last night were ringing with cheers for this magnificent event.

CHEERING   "BLOW AT REACTION"
THE NEWS   —GALLACHER
—REGARD my splendid vote and victory in West
of the policy of the

THE GOVERNMEN
WINS: LABOUI
VOTE GROWS

MacDonald Family
Rejected Flatly

THE result of the General Election is a vic National Government: but a victory offset by one increase in the Labour vote and the victo Gallacher, which shows the tremendous adv working-class unity.

Figures declared last night were 414 for the G 179 against.

The MacDonald family was wiped out at the t MacDonald, feeling, as he himself told rep platest down-in old man," was defeated at t by more than 20,000 votes.

Malcolm, his son, was heavily defeated at Bas Walter Elliot, Minister for Agriculture, just Kelvingrove with a majority of 149 on a full story of the Election, giving all outstand developments of the fight, appears on Pa

ATTLEE'S
MESSAGE

In a message limited last night, Mr. Attlee, leader of the Labour Party, said:

"The result of the election, although disappointing in terms of seats won, is disappointing. The seats gained might well have been increased by 10 or 70 per cent, with a very slight increase of votes.

"On the other hand, the totals of votes had show how great and widespread has been the response to Labour's policy of Socialism and peace.

"The fact is that the rising tide of Labour has again approached its previous high-water mark of 1929.

STATE OF PA

The State of the Parties up to the time of going to press was :—

Conservative	379
Liberal National	31
National Labour	8
National	2
FOR GOVT.	420

Labour	
Liberal	
Indepe	
Indepe	
Conn	
Indep	
FOR	

London was the home base of Sylvia Pankhurst's East London Federation of Suffragettes – at 400 Old Ford Road – as well as the base for WSPU (Women's Social and Political Union), relations with which became very strained when Sylvia started working with socialist organizations like the Herald League.

In 1913, Sylvia took the platform in support of Irish workers participating in the famous Dublin lockout. And this was the catalyst for Christabel Pankhurst, Sylvia's less radical sister, to finally break the link between the main group of the WSPU and Sylvia's East London Branch. While this East London federation of suffragettes argued forcefully that women's suffrage was just one step towards a full social and political emancipation that would entail a socialist state as its logical conclusion, the focus of this new movement that Kath found herself a part of was much more closely aligned with her views and growing political awareness.

Kids' protests

Kath was only too aware of the misery of slum living that clearly seemed to be a direct and logical consequence of the capitalist system and its failure to ensure for everyone decent housing, access to good education, fair pay, and health care. This part of London, with its diversity and revolutionaries, appealed to so many of Kath's social and political instincts.

Whilst she was a huge supporter of the Russian Revolution, it certainly caused some issues with fellow activists from the strong local Jewish community, as increasing numbers of Jews began to flee the anti-Semitic programs running across Russia.

Kath acquired new friends, Nellie and Rose Cohen, who, like Kath, would become lifelong political activists. Nellie had been captivated by suffragette speakers who seemed to appear on every street corner, and she eventually became Sylvia Pankhurst's personal secretary; Rose was quick to follow her sister and became an active member of the movement. Through her friendship with these remarkable sisters, Kath would become acquainted with their two comrades and flatmates. These were Daisy Lansbury, daughter of George Lansbury – who would later become the leader of the Labour Party – and the Irish feminist May O'Callaghan, who wrote for Pankhurst's paper *The Workers' Dreadnought* and, just like Kath, was well-read and had a lively sense of humor.

Kath found herself spending more and more time with the suffragettes and socialists at 400 Old Ford Road, a place which many government spies and later reports declared to be nothing less than a 'nest of revolution'. This was because, at this stage, the majority of the people there were communists, though Kath had not yet declared her allegiance to this cause.

Always interested in music, literature, and the arts, Kath also became involved with many literary and discussion groups, and thus she discovered and took a huge interest in the ideas of contemporary thinkers such as Sigmund Freud. She was part of the PLEBS, so-called after a magazine published by the National Council of Labour Colleges, which was, interestingly for the time, anti-Marxist. PLEBS, as a group, was formed with the modest aim of singing songs and performing sketches at meetings, and Kath, with her love of amateur dramatics, felt completely at home. Ironically, the most popular song in the short-lived PLEBS production repertoire was a song entitled 'Singing Jailbirds', an apt and prophetic title for what would happen in the coming years.

400 Old Ford Road, home of East London suffragettes

The suffragette movement had become a very different beast since its success in securing the vote for some women, in 1918. After the Russian Revolution of 1917, the movement was far from homogenous; and Sylvia's and Kath's left-wing suffrage group were increasingly becoming a minority within a minority.

Nellie and Rose, through their activism with Pankhurst, in 1919, set out, like others, to establish the British Communist Party. Their first public meeting was held at their flat on Greys Inn road, and Pankhurst put Nellie Cohen in charge of the new People's Russian Information Bureau. Funded by supporters of the Revolution, the objective was to counter negative media coverage by seeking to spread the 'truth' about Soviet Russia. Rose, again, would rise quickly through the ranks to take a high-profile position within the group, which would, by 1921, be funded by the Communist Party of Great Britain.

Kath and Rose were women campaigning at the highest level with the Communist Party but not yet members. Both were also great beauties, and while Kath was head-over-heels in love with Sandy and devotedly loyal, Rose became the love-interest of Harry Pollitt, the general secretary of the Communist Party. Becoming a communist in London in the 1920s provided a complete social identity, although the role of women and their position within the movement left much to be desired in terms of real equality, and the contribution of women to the cause was often undervalued in comparison with that of men. The fact that Kath and Sandy were in full-time employment as teachers made a real commitment by them to the party difficult, and though they would both join the Communist Party, it would not be until 1926 that Kath would truly commit to the ideology of a British Revolution.

In 1924, another Churchill came to Kath's Door, Dr. Stella Churchill, the newly selected Labour candidate to fight the seat of Hackney North. Like most of London's radical left, she was fully aware of Kath's success in running Churchill's parliamentary campaign in Dundee, in 1917. It is worth noting here, incidentally, that although Winston had secured over 80% of the vote with Kath's help, in 1917, by 1922 he had lost the seat to the very same opponent whom Kath had helped him defeat so roundly.

Both Kath and Sandy Duncan were huge supporters of Ramsey MacDonald, the current leader and a founding father of the Labour Party, so they were happy to turn their home over to the Party as Dr. Stella Churchill's election campaign office. Sadly, although the general election of 1924 would see Ramsey MacDonald lead the first Labour government in history, Dr. Churchill failed to win the seat of Hackney North, which is the very seat held today by Labour's Diane Abbott, the first black woman to be elected to parliament.

Nevertheless, 1924 brought some excitement to the Duncan household. MacDonald recognized the Soviet Union and offered loans to it. All seemed to be going so well, until the *Daily Mail* published what has become known as the Zinoviev letter scandal. This started to sow a seed in the mind of the public that the Labour Party was in bed with the Soviets. This, in turn, led to a no-confidence vote in MacDonald, and by 8 October, 1924, the first Labour government was out of office.

The Zinoviev letter, although widely regarded as the cause of the Labour defeat that year, was the subject of a critical historical review by former Labour Foreign Secretary, Robin Cook, in 1988. And in Jonathan Piles' well-researched book, *Churchill's Second Enemy*, it is alleged that the true source of the letter was M15, in particular, the secretive Sir George Joseph Ball and his colleagues.

It is ironic and depressing to note that, as I write this, in February, 2018, the front page of the *Daily Mail* and other right-wing newspapers carry stories, believed by some as scurrilous, alleging that the new leader of the Labour Party, Jeremy Corbyn, was a communist spy in the 1980s. It seems that even today, the view of the right-wing media is that hyping the fear of the Russian bogeyman is the best way to stop a progressive and popular Labour Party, currently at 40% in the polls, from getting its hands on the keys to Number 10.

In 2017, the Conservative government declared that it had 'mislaid' the original Zinoviev letter and the entire file relating to it, while failing to answer the question as to whether or not a copy of the letter and its file had ever been made.

By this time, Kath had mixed views on Ramsey MacDonald. Many on the left were accusing him of failing to do more to support the left's political agenda and deliver a truly socialist government. It was at this time that Kath and Sandy were given a copy of Lenin's *State and Revolution*, and it is their reading of this book that would make their politics more hardline and redefine them as communists.

In 1925, the *Sunday Worker* was launched as the voice of the left-wing movement, and Kath and Sandy would become two of its most loyal readers, supporters, and sellers at meetings and at factory gates. In the same year, they joined the Teachers' Labour League and a branch of the Workers' Theatre Movement, known as the People's Players, was set up in Hackney. Kath became a prominent and enthusiastic member, taking part in productions along with other high-profile political activists of the time.

In later years, she would feature as the primary subject of several plays written about her activism. I recently wrote a play about her, called Liberty, but this focuses on just one chapter in Kath's amazing life. And I have, as yet, been unable to trace any copies of the plays that were written about her during the 1930s. I would, therefore, be enormously grateful if someone were to be able to provide me with a copy or point me in the direction of an archived script.

1926 was the year of the General Strike, and it was this key event that led Kath and Sandy, who had been long-term members of the independent Labour Party, finally to join their comrades and become fully paid-up members of the British Communist Party.

It was certainly not a time to sit comfortably on the sofa and enjoy theoretical discussions; everyone was needed to help organize. Kath had had to change the way she fought her campaigns; London was very different from Scotland. When she had run Winston Churchill's by-election campaign, she had the use of theatrical sets and stages and had stood on trucks and cars with a loudhailer to get her message across to large crowds. In London, there was the constant fear of arrest; messages and propaganda for causes and campaigns were communicated by chalking slogans and details of meetings on walls and roads. Rallies would take place suddenly on any and every street corner, and Kath would unhesitatingly take the lead and rally others. Kath was extremely proud that her activism ensured that the 1926 General Strike was solid in her area and that no tram or bus moved in Hackney during the strike.

In 1928, Kath and Sandy, as leading members of the Friends of Russia movement and rising stars in the British Communist Party, travelled to the Soviet Union as part of the Teachers' Labour League delegation. Having helped establish one of the most active and successful communist party branches in the country, Kath found a warm welcome in Russia. It is almost certainly the case that, during this visit, the Russian secret service tried to induce Kath to spy for the Soviet Union. Kath had already declined advances from the British secret service to spy for them. She knew that both the Russian and British secret services were aware of her long and established friendship with Sir and Lady Winston Churchill, a friendship she valued highly. As a woman of very clear and set principles, the idea of spying on her friends and comrades was abhorrent to Kath, and this, just like all future advances from secret services and offers of employment as a spy, was politely but firmly declined. "You have my blood," she said, "my activism and my loyalty to the party; I think that says where my loyalties lie."

By 1930, it was time to establish the party and build the people's movement in another area of London. Kath had spoken in South London on many occasions and had strong links to it already, through her activism, while the area would make life easier, as it was closer to the places where she and Sandy worked. She felt that she had done all she could in Hackney, and Deptford was calling out for leadership. As usual, Kath stepped up to meet the challenge.

Chapter 3
The Hunger Marches

Coming home from school one day, Kath was confronted by a large object, wrapped in brown paper and sitting on the table, with her name on it. As it was neither her birthday nor Christmas. Kath was intrigued as to why this object was taking up most of the table space. At Sandy and Mama's request, she opened it up and all became clear: Sandy had found a large beer box, and knowing well both Kath's love of dramatics and the practicalities of street oratory, had painted on it, 'The Kath Duncan Stage' and attached a bright red ribbon as a handle so that it was easy to lift and carry or sling on her back.

Kath was, in every sense of the word, the leader of the unemployed in Deptford and across South London. But, activism and protest in South London was very different from working with Winston Churchill on his election campaign in Scotland, or campaigning with the suffragettes, who had proper stages and car bonnets to climb up on. Kath only had the pavements and street corners on which to speak, but she was just 5-feet-2-inches tall. Sandy, as usual, had come up with a practical solution. With her large beer box, Kath could perform and be clearly seen by everyone at the ever-increasing number of street rallies she conducted, and at the weekly rally on Deptford Broadway.

By 1926, the country had gone backwards since the mini-boom of the period after the war. Hunger, poverty, and unemployment again rose to record levels. And the Communist Party, still growing in popularity since its formation in 1920, was looking for a way to link all the pockets of support across the UK and mobilize tens of thousands in protest and civil unrest. Kath's oratory was becoming legendary, and whenever she took to her soapbox, it would not take long before hundreds, and eventually thousands, would gather to listen and rally to the Party's cause.

Kath Duncan with the Deptford Women's Reception Committee for the Hunger Marches

For Kath, this cause was unproblematic, but the way in which the Communist Party was beginning to seek to control her was becoming a problem. The party wanted to keep her and others on such a tight leash that it had begun to alienate the wider left – the Labour Party, the trades unions, and other groups. Kath always wanted all comrades and like-minded people working together for the common good and felt that real transformative power could only come in this way. But the party leadership saw things very differently. It would take almost another 10 years before the wider Labour movement and unions would begin properly to work together and speak with one voice.

Kath seemed not to have a single moment for herself. In fact, Kath's typical day seemed to be at least 26-hours long. And you wonder how and when she managed to get some sleep. While Mama kept the house running, Sandy would mobilize the comrades and do whatever errand Kath would ask of him. Kath would teach every morning and then spend the rest of the day selling the *Daily Worker*, chalking up on walls the details of the latest meeting or protest, and going from door to door collecting much-needed money to feed the desperate poor who filled her home day after day. Her efforts helped to fund the Hunger Marches, providing cash for food, accommodation, and medical costs, as well as occasional bail and police fines.

The Hunger Marches were started by the Communist Party in 1926, the year of the general strike in which Kath played such an important role. And they would continue on and off until 1936. Marching itself was just a small aspect of the National Hunger March Campaign and of the aims and objectives of the alliance of groups supporting it under a solidarity committee. In every town and village, a march passed through and meetings and rallies were held. Huge rallies would happen organically at factory gates where large numbers of workers and the unemployed could be found. All the time, the campaigners were collecting donations to fund the massive operation of bringing together so many marchers from every part of Britain.

There had always been friction between the National Unemployed Workers' Movement, organized by the Communist Party, and the TUC (Trades Union Congress), who were openly hostile to the Hunger March movement. And in 1928, relations deteriorated to such an extent that the Deptford and Greenwich Trades Council, which was affiliated to the London Trades Council, passed the following motion:

This council views with disgust the action of the T.U.C. general committee in repudiating the N.U.W.M. We take this as an act of treachery. We pledge ourselves to support the N.U.W.M. in their splendid work done on behalf of the unemployed. We instruct the secretary to get a statement of the work done by the Deptford Branch of N.U.W.M. and send same to T.U.C.

HUNGER MARCHERS LEAVE.

FAREWELL MEETING AT GREENWICH.

Prior to leaving for their home towns, representatives of the hunger marchers from Scotland, from Norwich, with the women marchers from Burnley, were entertained by the Greenwich and Deptford branch of the National Unemployed Workers' Movement on Friday evening.

After tea in the Co-operative Hall, High-street, Deptford, and the Reginald-road Hall, Deptford, a farewell demonstration was held at the Greenwich Baths, and in addition to the 80 hunger marchers there were between 1,500 and 2,000 others present.

Mr. Vic Parker, chairman of the Greenwich and Deptford branch, presided at the rally. The speakers included Mr. Fred Copeman, leader of the Norwich contingent, who was one of the sailors connected with the "Gordon" naval affair, Mr. Harry McShane, leader of the Scottish contingent, and Mrs. Kath Duncan, all of whom protested against the arrest of the "hunger" leaders, Messrs. Wal Hannington and Syd Elias.

The hunger marchers, who carried knapsacks and banners, arrived at the baths singing, and the meeting was quite orderly. A similar gathering was held at Rotherhithe Town Hall. After staying the night in a London institution the marchers left London on Saturday morning.

"CO-OP." DRAMATICS.

Under the auspices of the Education Department of the Royal Arsenal Co-operative Society, the Richidan Co-operative Players, on Saturday night, performed the farcical comedy, "Aunty Hasn't Know," at the Co-operative Institute, Parson's-hill, Woolwich. The hall was filled, and the play thoroughly amused the audience.

The players were as follows:—Aubrey Linton, ... Sidney Spiller, C. Leonard

The statement that followed read:

This branch was formed in October 1921 and since its inception has always given its whole-hearted support to every section of workers who have been in dispute. We were also responsible for getting from the Board of Guardians a decent scale of relief for the unfortunate people who were out of employment. During the Engineers Dispute, this branch did admirable work on behalf of the members of the unions concerned in this dispute. Our members acted as pickets and were responsible for stopping any black-legging in the area. We also were the means of getting the locked-out men relief for their wives and families. After the men went back to work, the branch received letters of congratulations from the Trades' union branches for the admirable work done on behalf of their members. We have also assisted other unions when they have been in disputes and, during the General Strike, our members worked night and day on behalf of trade unionists. We have a large percentage of our members who are members of their respective trade unions and we cannot understand the attitude of the T.U.C. towards this movement, and we think that they have been misinformed as to our aims and objectives. Our motto is 'Blackleg Proof' and we state quite categorically that none of our members has ever been guilty of black-legging on their fellow workers. We have always loyally assisted the Labour Party in every election that has taken place in this borough, and can state quite surely that, through our activities, we have been successful in maintaining Labour majorities on the Council, Guardians, and the London County Council. We have members in our ranks who are of all shades of opinion in politics, but they are all educated in the policy that injury to one is injury to all.

Despite such communications, it would not be until the 1930s that the Union movement and the Labour Party would work with the Communist Party to stand as one movement against injustice in all its forms.

Thanks to Kath, Sandy, and their fellow communist, Fred Copeman, Deptford was always at the forefront of organization and mobilization, setting up welcoming committees, and organizing food and accommodation for marchers from Scotland and other parts of the UK. Kath had wasted no time in using the docks as the key communicating link between the politically like-minded, reaching back to her hometown of Kirkcaldy and beyond, to the rest of the world.

In 1932, the National Union of Unemployed Workers led the calls for Deptford Borough Council to provide food and accommodation for the 300 marchers set to arrive in London that October. Large crowds greeted these men in Deptford as they marched in from Kent with their huge banners and chanted 'Down with the baby starvers', 'Down with the means test', and 'We don't want war, we want something to eat'. They were given local hospitality before the big march to Hyde Park on the following day to join the other marchers coming together as one movement from every part of Britain.

In September, 1933, Kath and Fred were tasked by the Communist Party to take the lead in organizing the Hunger March, from London, to the Trades Union Congress conference, in Brighton. They were at pains to make it clear that this was NOT an attack on the T.U.C but was instead part of a wider action that sought to bring together the entire Labour working class movement under The National Unemployed Workers' Movement's campaign, against the means test (welfare reforms). However, the T.U.C. did not want anything to do with the march, principally because of the rivalry between the two political parties; they banned it and forbade the 'official' unemployed associations, which existed in many areas, to support or take any part in it. The rank-and-file members of the T.U.C were enraged by this and were widely reported in the local press as being 'in revolt'. They ignored the ban and marched proudly with the N.U.W.M.

The march started with campaign rallies and meetings across London. Some 400-plus marchers left the embankment to loud cheers and the sound of Kath shaking her box for cash donations. Despite being unwell, she walked with as much of the march as she could, collecting and inspiring everyone along the route from London to Brighton, via Croydon, Redhill, and Crawley. This was, by hunger march standards, a short march; those marching from Scotland often spent five to six weeks on the road.

Vic Parker, one of the N.U.W.M organizers in South London, reported that, at Redhill, they had had to sleep in a freezing-cold sports stadium and that, by the morning, they were all half-frozen to death. The marchers were up at 6am to walk the last long stretch across open countryside, into Brighton. And with the sun beaming down on them for the last 26 miles, the marchers had gone from freezing to needing umbrellas to protect them from the blazing sun.

As the T.U.C had made it abundantly clear that they were not welcome in Brighton, it would have been easy for the weary Hunger Marchers to become despondent. However, they were tough and their spirits had been lifted by the huge crowds that had gathered to cheer them on and toss donations into buckets. At Croydon, local residents had organized a grand high tea with boiled eggs, whilst at Crawley, first-class accommodation and food were provided, with roast beef and potatoes, bread and butter pudding, and tea – a very rare treat. Other reports praised the shopkeeper in Streatham who had handed out baskets of apples to the marchers as they passed his shop, to help them on their way.

Lancashire contingent of Hunger Marchers, joined by Oxford undergraduates, October, 1932

Kath had become weak and exhausted but had been extraordinarily effective. The collections on the way to Brighton, and in the town on arrival, raised enough money to pay for all the marchers' train fares back to London.

Vic Parker wrote afterwards: *Kath did a magnificent job acting as treasurer of the march, and I well remember our staggering into a bank at Brighton with bags heavy with silver and coppers we had collected en-route.*

Will Hannington (second from left) outside Pentonville Prison, after serving a three-month jail sentence (note the package of letters he had not been allowed to receive until his release)

The T.U.C refused to welcome any of the marchers, despite pleas from delegates at the conference, and the block vote was used against them. The only comfort the marchers got were the cheers from the people of Brighton as they headed to the train station and home. Another attempt to unify the left had been missed, and bitterness would continue to prevail until 1934, when rank-and-file members would again march from London, with a different agenda from that of 1933.

While many people praised Kath Duncan and Fred Copeman for their organization of the 1933 London-to-Brighton Hunger March, there was far from harmony in the Party at large. The Croydon branch of the Communist Party published a statement which read:

'WE ACCUSE:

The Croydon local of the Communist Party of Great Britain has accused the London District party committee of failing to enforce party discipline, and of rank bureaucracy. We have accused Kath Duncan and Fred Copeman (leaders of the Brighton Hunger March) of financial unreliability, in as much as they have deliberately refused to pay their debts, despite their promises, and have issued a balance sheet calculated to put private individuals in the dock. Even the "Daily Worker" has failed to publish this balance sheet. The D.P.C. have suppressed the letters of the local which were sent to the party press. They refused to operate the majority decisions of this local, because they are afraid that they will lose some financial support. They give support to police, spies, opportunists, and careerists, yet they claim to be leaders, to lead the emancipation of the working class. We are compelled to use these methods because the party press has ignored our communications on the instruction of bureaucrats, yet the D.P.C. have stated in the Daily Worker *that the Chelsea group have misused the party press. And yet we are deliberately gagged. Why? We have been in communication with the Central Committee and they refer us back to the D.P.C., whom we have issues with. So much for party democracy!'*

Kath Duncan and Fred Copeman's leadership and honesty were not, and never had been, seriously in doubt. Political leaders throughout history, left and right, have been unjustly smeared. In any event, the Croydon branch produced no evidence of their allegations, and considering the high public profiles of both Kath and Fred, this accusation would have been a big story in the mainstream media at the time if there had been any suspicion of truth about it.

2,200 marchers were expected for the 1934 march, and accommodation and food needed to be found for them. With Kath and Sandy's strong links to Scotland, Deptford offered to accommodate 300 Scottish marchers, and a Southeast London conference was organized to make the arrangements. This conference took place in the Liberal Club, on New Cross Road, and the chair was another famous communist and political activist of the time, Tom Mann. He, like Kath, would go on to serve time in prison as a result of his seeking free speech and basic rights for workers. This meeting was ground-breaking in the diversity of groups that were represented. The *Daily Worker* wrote:

This conference was a landmark in the Working Class movement in Southeast London. The hall was packed with so many wanting to attend, the hall did not have the space. There were some 70 branches of 33 different working-class organizations such as Deptford No.2, A.E. Union, the Woolwich Trades Council, Co-Op, Guilds, Southwark Trade Union Committee, the Communist Party, The Independent Labour Party, the British Legion, the National League of the Blind, sports clubs, tenants associations, and unions brought together in a common struggle against the new Unemployment Bill, and in support of The National Congress and march.

This huge outpouring of support would have boosted Kath no end, but when the local reception committee asked for the Borough Council's help in accommodating the marchers, the council wrote back saying they had no suitable facilities that they could offer the marchers as accommodation. Kath was furious. It made no sense. For all the previous marches, the council had proved to be an exceptional host. Kath continued to put pressure on the council, until, on 21 February, just two days before the marchers were due to arrive in London, the following resolution proposed by the Deptford and Greenwich Trades Council was adopted and passed:

'*That we ask the Deptford Borough Council to support this Trades Council in their condemnation of the Unemployment Bill, as it throws new burdens on the local authorities, also that it fails to make unemployment insurance a national scheme.*'

This resolution was the first to bring the Trades Council and the Borough Council in line with the National Union of Unemployed Workers' Movement and the full aims and objectives of the 1934 National Hunger March. The Congregational Hall was offered as accommodation for the marchers, and the Labour County Council offered the Test Centre, on Nynehead Street, for the exclusive use of the organizers of the march; they also removed all restrictions from the march itself.

One of the Scottish marchers was invited by the Deptford and Greenwich Trades Council to speak about his own personal experience and about the importance of this march in particular. After he had spoken, the meeting passed a resolution of support and urged its members to mobilize all their membership in support of the campaign.

The following Sunday, Deptford was ready to march. 300 proud Scots – 302, including the ever-proud and inspirational Kath and Sandy Duncan leading local activists Peter Kerrigan and George Middleton – and a people's army of some two thousand marched with one voice on Trafalgar Square to link up with the tens of thousands marching on London from every corner of the land. They included an East-Anglian contingent from Norwich, which was led by Fred Copeman, who had just been released from jail.

The media coverage reflected the view of Parliament, that these people marching on London did not have any good intent and that trouble would follow. Rumors began to circulate that the army was being mobilized against the people, and that Wellington Barracks were being used for the first time for the mobilization of the Special Constabulary.

The marchers' petition – which, with over 1 million signatures, was the biggest petition in British history to date – was also becoming a huge issue. How could it be presented to Parliament? John McGovern, the Independent Labour Party MP for Gorbals, Glasgow, had offered to present it, but only a minority of committee members had agreed with this, arguing that it would enable the marchers to use the constitutional procedure of Parliament and thus make it far more difficult for the National Government, under Ramsey MacDonald, to refuse the petition. The overwhelming majority, including Kath, backed the motion that the marchers themselves should present the petition.

Kath and Fred arrived in Trafalgar Square on 27 October and mounted the plinth of Nelson's Column to speak to the largest crowd they had ever faced. Fred spoke of the pressing need to join the demands of the unemployed with the best interests of the employed and the Trades Unions. This was a position he shared with Kath, and which would become one of the biggest bones of contention within the Communist Party leadership, leading to the end of the N.U.W.M and removal of Wally Hannington from his role as a key member of the Party's executives.

As Fred and Kath and others spoke, the rally rapidly became ugly, with fighting breaking out across the Square between the police, some mounted on horses, and the marchers. All approaches to Buckingham Palace had been closed off, and although a delegation was permitted to get through the barrier to lobby the King, the staff at Buckingham Palace refused them access. The negative media coverage had sealed the fate of the march and its participants.

On Tuesday, 1st November, the day on which it had been decided to present the 1-million-signature petition to Parliament, reports of police brutality in Trafalgar Square were circulating widely. People were organizing local demonstrations and creating their own teams of marchers to march on Parliament from early morning until 8.30pm. Despite the police's attempts to suppress them, the crowds that turned out were much larger than those at the rally in Trafalgar Square on Sunday. Whitehall, Parliament Square, and the embankments east and west of the House of Commons were just one mass of angry people.

In the clashes with the mounted police and the newly mobilized Special Constabulary, reinforced by a huge number of additional officers from the Home Counties, four trams were overturned on the embankment and two cars set alight.

In the confusion, the solidarity committee decided to hide the petition at the Lost Property Office, at nearby Charing Cross Station. Fred raised concerns that this was the least safe option and that the petition should be carried openly, so that it could be seen by the maximum number of people who could also protect it.

When they arrived at the Lost Property Office to recover it, they discovered it had already been seized by the police, who refused to hand it back. Kath, Fred, and several others made a last effort to grab as many pages of the 1-million signatures as they could. Fred, the strongest, grabbed a bundle and fled, followed in hot pursuit by around a dozen police officers. Emerging from the underpass, Fred encountered a chaotic scene of rioting and was showered with glass from a canopy above the entrance to Trafalgar Square.

After the battles on the streets, John McGovern's speech in the House of Commons was somewhat flat. The police brutality and theft of the 1-million-signature petition, which brought months of hard work to nothing, left many feeling let down and critical of the leadership.

As always, nothing ever kept Kath down for long, and soon after the events at the House of Commons, she was taking part in the next direct action. She organized a fresh demonstration for the unemployed at County Hall as the Tory-led council were set to debate the means test and cuts to unemployment benefit. In Kath's eyes, these were savage, unnecessary cuts in all but name, and it was agreed that Kath would act as a decoy and lead a small deputation to the main entrance of County Hall from whatever point the police stopped the main crowd.

Meanwhile, another small group would come up on the riverside of the Hall and enter the Public Assistance Committee Room, from the balcony, a short time before the start of the committee meeting. Fred Abbott, an activist from Islington, Fred Copeman, and one other undertook this task. The police guarding the room did not notice as they took up their positions, and Fred and his team were already in place on the balcony as the members came into the room.

When the meeting turned to discuss the means test and cuts to unemployment benefit, the Labour members of the committee, as had been agreed, stood up in the constitutional fashion and opposed the scheme. At this moment, Fred and his accomplices climbed over the balcony and let themselves into the chamber reserved for council members only. The chair started banging on his desk, demanding order, while the leader of the Labour group, Herbert Morrison, pleaded with them not to do anything foolish. As pandemonium broke out inside the chamber, the police on duty were all outside the chamber, totally unaware of what was going on.

Fred Abbott started kicking over a few desks and chairs, while Fred Copeman sought to make clear to the councilors their concerns about the total injustice of the proposed cuts and present a London-wide petition against them and the other welfare reform proposals. The chair was sitting at a higher level than everyone else, and the petition was bulky and heavy. Fred, as a boxer, had a strong pair of arms and hurled the impressive bundle at the chair's desk. Unfortunately, it missed the desk and hit the chairman full in the face, knocking him out cold. It was at this point that the police became aware that things were not quite right within the chamber and entered onto a chaotic scene of overturned inkwells, upturned chairs, and desks scattered across the floor. The chair was out cold, surrounded by councilors trying to revive him, while the women present were all huddled together in one corner of the room. Fred Copeman, war hero, mutineer, and holder of the OBE, once again faced the courts and a prison cell.

The extensive charge sheet against Fred Copeman accused him of assaulting the chairman of the Statutory Committee, of obstructing the police in the carrying out of their duty (which happened to be their favorite charge at the time), of being on premises without the authority of the County Council, and of obstructing the proceedings of a properly constituted committee of the council.

The case was heard at Lambeth Police Court, and Kath rallied the unemployed, who packed the public gallery. Fred was sentenced to four months' hard labor in Pentonville Prison.

This prison stay would have a profound impact on Fred; his cell was close to the one which was used to hold convicted murderers before being hanged. This four-month period in jail would turn Fred into a lifelong activist against the death penalty. On his release, Kath and Sandy were on hand, as they always were, to take him home for one of Mama's breakfasts. He would later write that a man could never have hoped or wished for two better friends.

The National Unemployed Workers' Movement was the key organizing group within the Communist Party throughout the period of the Hunger Marches. The first national march was in 1922, and others followed in 1929, 1930, 1932 (which was the largest and remains the best known), and 1934. Many local Hunger Marches also took place. In 1935, 300,000 marched in South Wales; 160,000 in Glasgow; and tens of thousands in various areas, including Sheffield. And in 1936, there was the march from London to Brighton that I have already discussed. It is interesting that the Labour movement today is very selective in its historical memory and often chooses to forget its opposition to the Hunger Marches and the National Unemployed Workers' Movement, and focuses instead on the 'Jarrow Crusade' led by party officials.

No public demonstration greeted the Jarrow Marchers on arriving in or departing from London, but on the following day, Sunday, 8 November, 1936, a demonstration organized by Kath, Fred, and the N.U.W.M. leadership brought a staggering 250,000 people onto the streets. As the unsung Kath Duncan has proven, historians on the left and the right have chosen and continue to choose to be selective in their presentation of working-class history and its heroes.

In 1939, at the outbreak of World War II, the N.U.W.M disbanded and was finally dissolved completely in 1949. Although attempts were made to re-establish it in 1992, its time had passed.

Chapter 4
The Deptford Years

Kath's home in Deptford would always be open to all. Mama would be cooking continually, when she was not at church – she was the only person in the household who had a devout Christian faith. Well-beloved Butchers, on Deptford High Street, would always give her meat to feed the large number of people who would turn up at the house for food, advice, encouraging talks, and help and support with welfare and legal matters. Well-beloved Butchers still exists today, run by the same family. It has a new home on Tanners Hill, Deptford, and still makes the famous pies that are as loved today as they were in the 1930s.

Kath and Sandy had moved from Hackney to a very large and attractive house at 68 Ommaney Road, by Pepys Park, on Telegraph Hill. This house, it could be argued, would soon become one of the most important buildings in British working-class history, due to the caliber of the people who passed through its doors and the activism, local, UK-wide, and international, that was organized within.

Although Kath's love of literature was one of the things that had attracted her to the area – the playwright, Christopher Marlowe, had been murdered and buried here – Deptford, as dependent on its docks as Kirkcaldy was, had a history and heritage of global importance to the world as a major center of working-class struggle. Many important events had taken place here, including Wat Tyler's Peasants' Revolt, in 1381, when workers rose up against the King, Richard II, and his poll tax; Jack Cade's popular revolt against the corruption and abuse of power under Henry VI, in 1450; the Cornish Rebellion, in 1497, led by Michael Joseph, An Gof, against the high taxes that had been imposed on the people to pay for Henry VII's wars; and Wyatt's rebellion of 1554, when Wyatt, traumatized by the impact of the Spanish Inquisition, was seeking to stop Queen Mary from marrying Phillip of Spain. Many of Kath's revolutionary predecessors who had taken part in these and other events, had been tried and punished under treason laws.

However, when Kath arrived in Deptford, it is doubtful she could ever have imagined that she too would be tried and jailed under the same laws for taking on the power of the King, Parliament, and the entire legal establishment. She couldn't also have thought that she too would be the leader of her own famous Battle of Deptford Broadway and be the only woman to be charged with sedition over the past hundred years. She could not have predicted that she would be interviewing men who wished to fight for the Spanish Republic during the Spanish Civil War, while at the same time raising money to buy an ambulance to keep safe the very people she was sending to fight.

However, she would have been only too aware of the importance of the black slave Olaudah Equiano and his writings and activism. Equiano had been kidnapped in Deptford and sold as a slave, in a way not dissimilar to that of Solomon Northup. This means his story finally achieved the recognition it deserved after being told in the 2013 film, *12 Years a Slave*. Kath, just like this important leader of the anti-slavery movement in the UK, would, on her death, become yet another working-class hero whose activism and heroism would be parked well in the shadows.

44 Waller Road, Deptford

Kath was more than ready to accept the challenge of a different location and taking a new direction. She was still teaching at the same school, Battersea Day Continuation School, and as Deptford was so much closer, living there would give her more time for her activism. Sandy, who was also teaching at a local Bermondsey school, would also save time and walk to work from their large Victorian terrace house, at 68 Ommaney Road. This house would rapidly become the center for Kath's increasing circle of friends, comrades, and activists, all of whom were united in seeking to bring about the revolution.

Deptford Broadway bustled with life and, with its trams, trains, and buses, and sheer diversity, was like no other place Kath had seen before. Its wonderful theatres and movie house were wonders to behold, but the greatest draw was the famous Deptford market. Kath could spend hours there, receiving shouts of 'Good on ye', Kath' as she went about her business. The rights of the traders were very much in her heart, and she enjoyed the banter and the earthiness of the crowd.

68 Ommaney Road, probably the most important house in working-class history

Deptford's main street had had barrows for centuries, and with Kath around, no one was going to lose their livelihood because of gentrification. Therefore, when the market came under threat, Kath was not just the first point of call, she was way ahead of the game in organizing her response. The market traders, supported by the shopkeepers, set up a fighting fund to defend the market. Kath took up the baton, chalking up her concerns and mobilizing the locals. As the recognized leader of Deptford in all but name, she held a street meeting to plan a line of open protest and then spoke on behalf of the traders at the council offices. To make it clear that this was a campaign that she and the locals would win, in her usual vigorous style, Kath mobilized the traders, local residents, and the unemployed, and anyone else she could muster to march on the council. It was no surprise that the council backed down, and Deptford market, still poorly served by Lewisham Council, in 2018, continues to this day.

Moving from Hackney also caused Kath a significant personal sacrifice: she had to give up the amateur dramatics she loved and the supportive network of fellow activists she had built up and go it alone. Her acting, though, had given her the confidence to stand on any street corner or at any factory gate and address the hecklers and non-believers, as well as the many who, inspired by her words, were ready to march with her and take on active roles in the Party and the wider movement.

Grove Street, Deptford

Although Deptford had its theatres, it lacked its own dramatics society, and so Kath and Sandy's home soon accommodated what would become Deptford's answer to the Hackney Players. Her new dramatics society was called 'The Red Blouse W.T.M. Group'. To be a member, acting ability, it was said, was only of secondary importance; much more important was a modicum of courage and the determination to overcome nerves.

Workers had been and continued to be conditioned against artistic expression – due in part to the hatred of art by the money-grabbers of the 19th century, Matthew Arnold's 'philistines' – and it took real courage to go out on the streets and put on a show, although the works of Marlowe would have been a bit too high-brow for the 'Red Blouses'. Reports of their activities state that they 'drilled' rather than rehearsed. They would claim they were more inhibited than the Germans. They saw their productions very much along the line of agit-prop and Brechtian in nature, and their intention was to take a truly people's theatre to the masses, rather than to expect audiences to come to them.

The 'Red Blouses' would perform on the streets, in co-op halls, Trades' union halls, factories, pits, and labor exchanges; there was no carrying of cumbersome lighting equipment, props, or costumes; they saw themselves as truly, 'a property-less theatre for a property-less class'. Their productions drew large crowds because their productions dealt with issues, problems, and tragedies of everyday life and gave powerful voice to the feelings of ordinary men and women. Their inspiration was utterly Brechtian: 'When the workers themselves were artistically creative, they were thrilling and original'.

After the Battle of Deptford Broadway, the players performed a potted history of the event, staged at Greenwich Borough Hall, on Royal Hill. The script had been hurriedly put together and the play, terribly under-rehearsed, as usual, was performed during the remand week to help collect money for the fighting fund and raise the profile of the injustice of the entire case. Sandy Duncan, for example, who had been badly beaten in the battle, was sitting on the stage, his head bandaged, and this gave the players the opportunity to demonstrate to the spectators the sheer brutality of the police's treatment of their comrades.

They would also relate the play to the real anger around imperialism and its wars. One of the characters in the play took the line that at least war meant work, which gave the other performers the chance to explain, in full, the nature of modern war and expose the motives of the drive to war and the real scenes of death and destruction that were being prepared. It was at street theatre like this, and at similar events such as Kath's weekly rallies, that the wider working-class public could gain critical insight and perspective on the big issues of the day.

The Deptford Communist Party, under Kath's leadership and activism, rapidly became the largest Communist Party branch in the country, and certainly the most active; something that would prove consistently problematic to the powers of the state. The poverty and slum housing were at odds with the huge amount of affluence that was visible in Deptford in the 1930s.

In 1931, there was great excitement after plans were published to sell the house at 34 Albury Street, Deptford, which had been the home of Lord Nelson for the last five years of his life.

One of Deptford's theatres in the 1930s

The plan was to sell his house to America. Glossy American magazines carried advertisements waxing lyrical about the doors made from timber from ships commanded by the famous admiral, H.M.S. *Victory* and H.M.S. *Bellerophon*; the stair banisters of Jacobean oak; the woodcarvings by Grinling Gibbons; and the chain protruding from the left doorpost, which had been part of the Victory's anchor chain.

At the time, the house was being used by the Deptford Babies' Hospital and could accommodate just 18 cots. The hospital was so overwhelmed with babies needing to be looked after that 34 Albury Street had become simply too small and larger premises had to be found. Despite all the hype, Kath said the Americans would not be so stupid as to buy it, and they did not, and Kath supported the Hospital in many ways until it finally moved to Breakspear Road, in Brockley.

On making this discovery, I rushed back to Deptford and what a delight it was to see that 34 Albury Street still remains to this day, in all its splendor – although, like much of Lewisham Borough's heritage – with not so much as a blue plaque to tell you.

Kath was spoilt for choice when it came to social issues that needed to be tackled in Deptford, but she started with what she already knew, building support for the hunger marches and selling the *Daily Worker* on Deptford Broadway, where she would hold weekly rallies that attracted very large crowds. She then went out and about, at the gates of factories and of the labor exchange, and at every location where a crowd could be found. She worked tirelessly to ensure that local children could get food and held the council to account in every respect in order to care for her people in Deptford. Her power to inspire others was immense. Margaret Kippen, who was just a young girl at the time, reported many years later:

"We would hang about on the edge of the crowd when Kath Duncan was holding one of her weekly meetings. We did not understand what it was all about, but there was a sense of excitement, especially when there was barracking from the crowd. Like most out-door speakers, Kath was on the receiving end of plenty of such heckling, especially in the early years. Bill Jones remembers Kath as a small woman making powerful speeches outside the Lord Clyde pub; all the young lads who had managed to find tuppence for a glass of beer would heckle her. As a distinctive and colorful character, Kath acquired the inevitable nicknames, the two most common being 'The Red Herring' and 'Kath Bunkham'."

Deptford Broadway looking towards Blackheath, 1930s

Bert Gilpin, in his brief booklet, *Sketches from the Life of a Proletarian*, remembers one dark November evening when he set off to meet up with his father, who was active in the Labour Party and attending a meeting at the Labour Hall. When he arrived, he could not find his father but was handed a leaflet from the Communist Party, who were also holding a meeting inside the hall. The speaker, he reports, was a strong-looking woman from Deptford, called Kath Duncan, and:

She cleared all my doubts as to what socialism was and how the workers were going to win it. When the chairman asked anyone wishing to join the Communist Party to see the secretary at the end of the meeting, I was quickly there and said that this was what I had been looking for all my life.

This was in the 1930, and the usual probation period of one month for party membership was set aside when Bert disclosed that he was the son of old Jonnie Gilpin. Days later, he joined Kath and other comrades on the High Street, selling copies of the *Daily Worker* and speaking with the unemployed outside the labor exchange. Deptford Broadway rapidly became the weekly meeting spot. It was here that news could be obtained, and it was here that protests would start and finish.

68 Ommaney Road rapidly became a place of interest for MI5 and other organs of state power. In Hackney, Kath had been just one of many activists who lived in a house the police regarded as a place of 'revolution', but in Deptford, she was turning into a very different problem. As she was a friend of the Churchills, who had an extensive network of other powerful acquaintances, it had been all the more alarming that she refused their invitation to become a state spy. Instead, she turned her and Sandy's home not only into a house of revolution, but, in their words, a house of 'deviants', due to the large numbers of gay and transvestite people who were welcomed and used Kath's home essentially as a social club.

Kath could understand workers being jailed for standing up to the system and people being punished for public protests and activism, but she could not understand why increasing numbers of her friends were being jailed and sentenced to hard labor just because they loved or were attracted to people of the same sex. Kath would always stand by and support her gay friends, even when others, including their own families, abandoned them. She gave them food, a place to sleep, and encouragement to stand up for their rights, even if speaking out would lead to a longer prison sentence or additional hard labor.

One such friend was Percy Duke, who, when he was 40-years-old and living with Kath, was arrested for being found in an enclosed (private) garden at 30 Bishops Thorpe Road, Sydenham. He was further charged by the police for persistently importuning for immoral purpose. Duke pleaded guilty to the charge after the police produced evidence that he was dressed in full female attire as he went in and out of the gardens. Initially, the police had believed, on account of the figure's erratic behavior, that it was a woman who had escaped from a mental hospital and asked, "Are you in trouble, Miss?"

Thereupon, Duke lifted his skirt, the officer claimed, and replied, "Will you do my suspenders up? Are you coming my way?" Just as another constable arrived at the scene, Percy was reported as running off but was quickly caught. During a body search, the police reported finding ladies' cosmetics and two papers containing indecent writing. It is not known exactly what it was; the reporting at the time clearly wanted to give the impression that it was too indecent to publish, but it could have been no more than a man's name.

NELSON'S LAST SHORE HOME.

Deptford House for America ?

The above is an illustration of No. 34, panelled halls. Examples of the former [...]bury-street, Deptford, where, it is can be seen in the picture. [...]d, Lord Nelson, of Trafalgar fame, The chain which is shown hanging by [...]ssed the last five years of his life which the door of No. 47 is claimed to be from [...] spent ashore. the Victory's locker.

Duke did not want to get Kath mixed up in his situation and refused to confirm his address, saying he was a traveler and had concussion of the brain. Kath was furious when she discovered that the courts had given him six months' hard labor. He could easily have been physically or mentally unwell, but in the eyes of the state, it seemed, nothing was worse than being gay or transvestite. Handing out excessively harsh sentences was justified, in the state's mind, if it succeeded in stamping out, what was in their view, an abominable and 'deviant' practice.

Kath herself would be arrested and charged, for the first time, in December, 1932. Many people who have written about Kath's life have often missed the fact that she was jailed twice; first in 1932, and second in 1934, after the high-profile court case following her arrest on 30 July that year, which I cover in a later chapter.

In 1932, a local newspaper, the *Kentish Mercury*, reported that,

'A sensation was caused in Greenwich and Deptford districts on Monday when it became known that a leader of the unemployed and the Communist Party candidate at the 1931 general election for Greenwich had been arrested.'

The court described Kath Duncan as 44 years of age, married, of Ommaney Road, New Cross. The allegation against her was that, on 14 December, 1932, she was 'a disturber of the peace of our lord, the King, and an inciter of others to commit crimes and misdemeanors'. It would be the very same charge that would be brought against her again on 30 July, 1934.

Kath was beautifully turned out for the trial, as she always was, and the press reported as much about how she looked as the words she spoke. With respect to her appearance in the dock, we are told that the accused was wearing a black leather coat, with an astrakhan collar and matching hat. And it is written that she stood smiling at Tower Bridge Police Court as Detective Inspector Renshaw, of the Special Branch, asked for a remand to enable the Director of Public Prosecutions to be present. The magistrate (Mr. Campion) asked Kath if she objected to being put on remand, to which she replied, "I do. I wish to be tried at once. You've brought me here, and I want to know the charge."

Inspector Renshaw said he would not object to bail if the prisoner would give an undertaking not to speak at or attend any political meetings before the case was heard, but Kath refused to give any such undertaking and bail was denied. Mr. Campion said, "Then the case must be put back until the Director of Public Prosecutions can be contacted to appear. It is only right the case against the woman should be dealt with as soon as possible."

The case was then put back by an hour, after which Kath was brought back into the dock and Mr. E. Clayton appeared for the Director of Public Prosecutions.

The subject of complaint, said Mr. Clayton, was in some of the words used by the accused in a speech at a meeting of the National Unemployed Workers' Union, at Bermondsey Town Hall. It was a speech, he said, "Calculated to create a breach of the peace," and, "the defendant seems to have taken a very prominent part, having spoken for half an hour." The specific object of the complaint, he said, was that, in this speech, the defendant had said that:

The Public Assistance people should be identified and their addresses found, in order that pressure could be bought to bear on them. It is the duty of the workers to do this. Every member of a local Public Assistance committee who refuses relief to unemployed men or who wants to send an unemployed man to Belmont Prison must be identified and addresses got, so that they can be intimidated.

The Director of Public Prosecutions considered that these words were calculated to provoke a breach of the peace and that there was no doubt that the accused had personally endeavored to carry out these threats.

Witness for the prosecution, Detective Inspector Jones, of the Special Branch, said he was at the meeting on 14 December, 1932, at Bermondsey Town Hall. There were about 200 people present and the defendant and two others spoke. He admitted that he did not take shorthand notes of her speech at the time but later jotted down parts of her speech which struck him as being most important.

In her address, she compared the Public Assistance committees and the old Guardians and said that, whereas the workers could elect the Guardians, who were local people and amenable to pressure, the officials of the Public Assistance committees were unacquainted with local conditions. They were hard and did not sympathize with the working class. As they were unknown, they could walk about the streets with impunity. It was, she continued, the intention of the National Unemployed Workers' Union to find out the names and addresses of these people, in order that pressure might be bought to bear on them, through demonstrations to be held outside their houses and places of business. The detective added that she also said, *'Any person who cuts down an unemployed person's scale of relief (welfare income) or orders them to Belmont Prison must be intimidated until they go in fear of their lives.'*

Kath, conducting her own defense, challenged Detective Inspector Jones on his assertion that it would look odd taking notes at a public meeting, when the gallery was full of reporters taking notes. His excuse, that he did not want to draw attention to himself, did not ring true, said Kath. Also, who, after hearing a 30-minute speech, can then write it up accurately after the event? Although the magistrate said that he himself had made notes from memory in similar circumstances, Kath firmly denied the charges against her.

A new witness was called to give evidence, Detective Sergeant Phillips, from New Scotland Yard. He said that the defendant had addressed a meeting at Southampton Street, Camberwell, on 18 December, 1932, and that he had seen her again at a demonstration outside the works of a Mr. Evan Cook, a borough councilor at Hollydale Road, Peckham. Mr. Cook was also a member of the Public Assistance committee, and it was alleged that demonstrators who had been refused access to his premises then yelled out abuse and filthy words before marching on Camberwell Town Hall. Kath again challenged the allegations against her, saying that she had, in fact, telephoned Mr. Cook in advance and that he had agreed to meet her delegation.

As the case ended, the magistrate asked Kath if she would prefer to give evidence or a statement from the dock, but Kath, being Kath, chose to make a speech:

'I want to completely deny that I used the words complained of. What I said was that it was necessary for the unemployed workers to get the names and addresses of the members of the Public Assistance committee so that we can bring pressure – local pressure – to bear on them. When, on Friday, demonstrators went to see Mr. Cook, the police refused us admission. I went to the telephone box and decided with the vice chairman of the Public Assistance committee to meet him. He expressed his willingness to meet me and members of the unemployed, and this was carrying into practice what I had preached, and this was the whole purport of my speech, as I had brought pressure to bear on him to get him to meet with us. It is true the police were brought into the building while I was there, but not at the request of the vice chairman. If he had

thought I was doing anything that was not perfectly legitimate, he could have called in the police at any time and have me turned out. No one would be so foolish as to use the words attributed to me in any public speech. What I said was perfectly legitimate and had been said again and again. We want to bring pressure to bear on the members of the Public Assistance committee and it must be obvious to everyone that this is a perfectly legitimate remark to make about local members.'

When, before making his ruling, the magistrate asked whether there was anything known about the accused, Renshaw informed him that the accused had been active in local public life for five years and that she had never been in trouble before. The magistrate then told Kath that he would be willing to take the accused's word that no such conduct would happen again and would bind her over to her own recognizances to keep the peace for six months. When Kath asked what would happen if she refused, she was told that she would have to find a surety of £50 to keep the peace for six months or go to jail. The inevitable consequence of Kath sticking to her guns ensued, and she was jailed for the first time.

Years of being a friend of the Churchills meant that MI5 had to take real care over Kath. While most people were kept very much in the dark about their friendship, the British state, Russia, the Communist Party, and most MPs in Westminster were fully aware of it. However, there is no evidence at all that Kath ever sought to use this friendship for political or personal gain, although others might well have done.

After the Battle of Deptford Broadway, Sandy was the only member of the group that the police called 'troublesome and violent ringleaders' not to be jailed. It is interesting to speculate, on the basis of questions raised in the House of Commons, as to the reasons why Sandy Duncan was not jailed or sacked from his job as a teacher for the London County Council. Sir Winston Churchill certainly was well aware that, if Sandy were jailed, as well as Kath, it would leave them destitute. It is an interesting theory that, on this occasion and on others, he was working behind the scenes to ensure that Sandy never went to jail. Kath, due to her outspokenness and her position as a leader, could not be saved from jail, but it is certainly at least possible that Churchill employed a quiet word to ensure that she received a more lenient sentence than she might have otherwise received.

DEPTFORD PRISONERS' "WELCOME HOME."

COMMUNIST MEETING IN THE BROADWAY.

"Our boys have come out of prison better fighters than ever," declared Mrs. Kath Duncan, the Greenwich Communist leader, at the meeting held in Deptford Broadway, on Wednesday, to welcome back the men who were sentenced to four months' hard labour in connection with the unemployed disturbances in the Broadway on June 12th—George Childs (24), clerk, of Vesta-road, Brockley, and Albert Sydney Crane (24), hosier, of Shere-road, Deptford. The prisoners, who were released from Brixton gaol at nine o'clock that morning, were given a rousing cheer from a section of a crowd of about 300. A red banner which surmounted the "platform"—a cart—bore the words "Welcome Home to Our Class War Prisoners" and another beneath stated that "Neither Brixton Nor Belmont Will Break Us."

Childs, in thanking the "comrades" for the welcome, said he wanted them to know that he and Crane were coming back into the movement fighting fit and were going to put every ounce of energy into their fight.

"We only got four months," said Crane, "but we might have got six had it not been for your pennies and twopences. We hope you will all come in and fight with us. If you had all been with us we would not have been sent to gaol."

"It's a long time since I felt so happy and excited standing on a working-class platform," said Mrs. Duncan, "because ever since our boys were sent down we have had a real gap in our movement. Now we have got them back with us in such excellent fighting spirit we know we are going to be very much stronger and do much better work in the strenuous times that are facing the working classes." Referring to the West Ham riots, she said, "What West Ham can do we surely can do—not that we are anxious to get any one's head coming close contact with a police baton, but the more stronger and powerful we become the less fear is there of a police baton being brought into operation."

The other two prisoners—MacCafferty and Lucas—will be released from Brixton to-morrow morning and will be similarly welcomed.

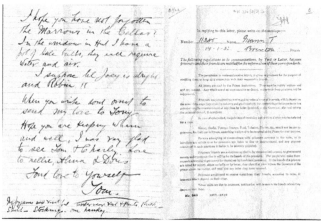

I hope you have not forgotten
the Marrows in the Cellar?
In the window in that I have a
lot of little balls, they will require
water and air.
I suppose lil Joey is alright
and Robin is

When you write send ours to
send my love to Tony
Hope you are keeping Warm
and well, I was very glad
to see Tom & Charley. Love
to Nellie, Alma & Doris

Fond love to yourself
Tom.

Letters from Tom Mann to Mam, Kath Duncan's mother, about Kath's poor health, from Brixton Prison, in which he was held the same time as Kath

Chapter Five
Civil Rights and the Battle of Deptford Broadway

The arrest and jailing of Gandhi was national news; the high-handed treatment of this peaceful protestor justly caused international outrage. However, the arrest and jailing of pensioner and communist Tom Mann for simply demanding free speech and civil rights went largely unreported. After all, since the suffragettes, the prison system had been reliant on the influx of civil-rights protestors and gays as its staple daily intake, and this was not going to change any time soon.

Kath, from her early years, had seen the impact that even the shortest of prison sentences could have on people's wellbeing. She had known fellow suffragettes to be force-fed and cruelly treated by the state in other ways. And the abuse and punishment of people for just being homosexual, or for demanding basic civil rights, was utterly incomprehensible to her.

In the autumn of 1931, the Japanese invaded Manchuria. The position of the British government seemed to be that, as long as it was not an attack on the British Empire, it was not something the British government should interfere with. After all, British scrap merchants – who were shipping waste they would otherwise have found difficult to dispose of, to help with the Japanese war effort via London's docks – were making fortunes out of it.

It was the Communist Party that led the call for action, and as usual, their campaign was designed by Kath and her growing band of communist agitators. They planned a series of marches from Deptford Broadway to Beresford Square, in Woolwich, near to the docks.

Every weekend, Kath led her 'merry men and women' through the Blackwall tunnel, and hundreds of workers from the riverside boroughs marched with them through the docklands, calling on dockers not to load the 'murder ships' that were carrying British war materials and weapons to Japan.

However, the march on 12 June, 1932, was very different. As usual, the march was chaperoned by a police inspector who, as contemporary reports state, was on this occasion decidedly not in their favor and, whilst in Woolwich, was seen in many of the local pubs, soothing his feelings. It is certain that his temper was not improved by the long march back to Deptford and the subsequent battle that would take place on his watch.

After Kath and Sandy had spoken to a 3,000-strong crowd in the anti-war demonstration at Woolwich, a small but tired group of marchers from Deptford arrived back at Deptford Broadway, at around 11:30pm. What happened next would go down in London's history as the Battle of Deptford Broadway. On the site of so many previous battles for social justice, Kath was about to mount the stage of history with her own battle of the people against the unjust use of power by the state.

Slet   July-2...34   4

Kath Sinclair
DUNCAN.
Police Court.

301/MP/1994.

          Kath Sinclair DUNCAN, a school teacher, of
68 Ommaney Road, S.E., appeared at Tower Bridge Police
Court at 10 a.m. this day to answer a charge of "wilfully
obstructing Inspector William Jones, a constable of the
Metropolitan Police Force, whilst in the execution of his
duty, at Rynehead Street, S.E., on the 30th July, 1934,
etc".

          When she stepped into the Dock she immediately
asked the Learned Magistrate - W. H. Oulton, Esq., - for
a remand to enable her to prepare her defence and obtain
legal aid.   Objection was raised by prosecuting counsel
on the grounds that the case was a simple one of obstruction
of a police officer, and that it required no elaborate
defence.   Duncan responded that she wished to call
witnesses to rebut the anticipated evidence of police and,
during the short time at her disposal since her release
on bail yesterday, she had had no time to get into touch
with them.

          The Magistrate accordingly granted a remand
in Duncan's own recognisances of £5, until Monday next,
6th August, at 10.30 a.m.

          I am informed that the Council for Civil
Liberties will endeavour to make this an important case
and will brief counsel for the defence.

          In view, however, of the nature of the charge
which cannot truthfully be denied, it is almost certain

31st   July   4

Kath Sinclair

DUNCAN.

Police Court.

801/MP/1934.

           Kath Sinclair DUNCAN, a school teacher, of
68 Ommaney Road, S.E., appeared at Tower Bridge Police
Court at 10 a.m. this day to answer a charge of "wilfully
obstructing Inspector William Jones, a constable of the
Metropolitan Police Force, whilst in the execution of his
duty, at Nynehead Street, S.E., on the 30th July, 1934,
etc".

           When she stepped into the Dock she immediately
asked the Learned Magistrate - W. R. Oulton, Esq., - for
a remand to enable her to prepare her defence and obtain
legal aid.   Objection was raised by prosecuting counsel
on the grounds that the case was a simple one of obstruction
of a police officer, and that it required no elaborate
defence.   Duncan responded that she wished to call
witnesses to rebut the anticipated evidence of police and,
during the short time at her disposal since her release
on bail yesterday, she had had no time to get into touch
with them.

           The Magistrate accordingly granted a remand
in Duncan's own recognisances of £5, until Monday next,
6th August, at 10.30 a.m.

           I am informed that the Council for Civil
Liberties will endeavour to make this an important case
and will brief counsel for the defence.

           In view, however, of the nature of the charge
which cannot truthfully be denied, it is almost certain

that a conviction will ensue.

Duncan was met outside the Court by her husband, Ronald KIDD and Ken HARVEY. Ronald KIDD, after a short consultation with Duncan, drove away in motor car Index No. Y.M.8389. The Duncans and Harvey took refreshment at a local public house and then departed by tram for Greenwich.

No attempt was made to demonstrate outside the police court, where not more than twelve persons were assembled.

I have been told that, in this campaign of the N.U.W.M. against the police ban on meetings outside labour exchanges, the instructions to speakers are for them to abstain from incitement of the audience which would result in a physical clash with police.

William East.

Sergeant.

Submitted.

W. Hay.

Inspector.

Superintendent.

As they arrived back in Deptford, the protesters were singing *The Internationale* as they marched, though they would always refrain from singing as they passed the hospital.

Once the crowd had reached Deptford Broadway, Kath, as usual, mounted her soapbox stage and delivered another impassioned speech, surrounded by red flags and placards bearing the usual range of contemporary slogans. As she was coming to the end of her speech, the police inspector who had been chaperoning the march – and, by this time, had clearly had too much to drink – called for more police reinforcements. They subsequently arrived in large numbers on horseback and in vans, armed with batons and shields. They immediately demanded that the marchers stop singing and disband. Kath was told to stop preaching revolution and the protestors were asked to surrender their arms.

In the police's view, the poles they were using to carry the flags and slogans counted as weapons. Kath spoke out, saying that they were just peaceful workers and residents of Deptford who were simply meeting as comrades to share news and solidarity and who had no violent intentions: "What you claim are weapons," said Kath, "are just poles to carry our thoughts, and no more."

The police then charged with batons and shields, and 'The Battle of Deptford Broadway' ensued as the police began savagely to beat men, women, and children, including the high-profile activist, Alf Lucas, and Sandy Duncan. Many were dragged by their hair into the back of police vans and others beaten so savagely that they could not stand up. Vanload after vanload of peaceful protestors were hauled off to prison cells.

Kath called out to her comrades to link arms and not fight back. "To fight them is to make us no better than them!" she called out, and led the crowd in singing *The Red Flag*. People carried on singing as the blows rained down on them; blood running in the street and covering everyone's clothing in imitation of the color of the flags they carried and the song they were singing. Sandy was so badly beaten that he was rushed to hospital, as were many others. When the police had carried away as many as they could to jail, and were themselves exhausted from the beatings they had given out, Kath still stood, covered in blood – the red of the blood grimly matching the red of her hair. She was surrounded by her small blood-splattered group of loyal comrades who formed a protective shield around her.

Kath helped her comrades back to 68 Ommaney Road and then set about knocking up comrades door-to-door, asking them to take their rent books and what little cash they had to Blackheath Hill Police Station to bail out as many as they could of their many comrades who had been arrested. Mama had food on the stove and was already on the doorstep, scrubbing the front steps, which had been stained with the blood of fleeing protestors.

The next few days would be spent in raising money for the support fund and for the legal defense of those protestors who had been jailed and fined and in producing shirts carrying pictures of those who had been arrested and beaten.

On the following day, Monday, 13 June, as news circulated as to what had gone on, there was huge indignation across Deptford at the injustice and police brutality. The men in the two test and work centers, training centers for the unemployed, came out on strike. And by the evening, a crowd of over 5000 had gathered on Deptford Broadway as Kath, again on her soapbox, denounced the unprovoked attack and demanded that the police inspector who had instigated it be dismissed. The authorities were not willing to give any ground, and the police, reinforced by a mounted division brought in especially, tried to break up the justly angry demonstrators. Previously, Kath had ordered the protestors not to fight back; this time, however, they did, and they succeeded in scattering the police.

On the following morning, Tuesday, 14 June, the people of Deptford were still angry that they were living in what seemed to be a police state, in which a police officer could invent any charge he liked because no magistrate would find against him. This sense of injustice fueled their anger all the more.

All day long, large crowds were on the streets of Deptford and Greenwich, declaring their solidarity with street meetings and cash collections for the defense of the prisoners. The reporter for the *Daily Worker* who was covering the unrest reported that '*There are groups of police patrolling about, and the place (Deptford) feels like an armed camp.*'

Things continued like this for the whole week, with huge numbers of people on the streets, speakers on most corners, and contributions from most of the local unions and organizations pouring into the defense fund. 100 extra police were drafted in to keep the peace, but the protestors were disciplined and well-behaved under Kath's leadership. Stewards were recruited to keep order and make sure that everyone was well informed; and this ensured that no further battles would follow, at least for the time being.

Kath, as always, was the leading spirit in this campaign. While so many men were in custody or hospital, she saw to it that everyone was fully supported and their battle for liberty would not go without a champion. Alf Lucas was quoted as saying, 'It was like the General Strike all over again. Deptford and Greenwich were alive with news.'

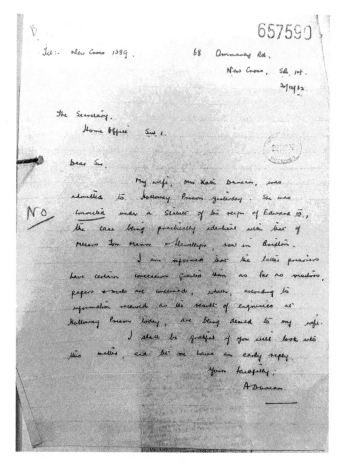

Kath's defense fund raised £90, a huge sum of money for the time, and some people had even made donations of £1 notes, a staggering sign of generosity.

As the men were being brought before the magistrates, large crowds attended the courts and the prisons, walking and standing in the pouring rain to cheer in support. When the men were released, receptions were laid on at Greenwich Baths, sometimes with a full breakfast provided, which was a real treat, as most would have been grateful for just a slice of bread and dripping. The people of Deptford and Greenwich had done what Kath had longed for all her political life: they had all come together – communists, unionists, militants, workers, and women – to fight for a better life for the poor and unemployed, for their civil rights, and against capitalist war.

George Lansbury, the leader of the Labour Party, which was in opposition at the time, was getting increasingly alarmed at the constant arrest of civil-rights activists. Tom Mann, a worker from Battersea – leading communist and veteran unionist – had just been jailed, leading Lansbury to declare in parliament, 'Of all the tomfool laws to apply in modern times, this one takes the biscuit.' Criticizing the presence of police detectives at public meetings, he made it clear that, 'It's no business of the police to know what any of the citizens are thinking about; let them mind their own business and look after burglars.'

A Conservative MP, Captain A.L.S. Todd, raised this question in the House of Commons:

'Was the Minister of Education aware, that Mrs. Kath Duncan, an L.C.C. teacher, was only cautioned by the L.C.C. education committee following her sentence, and is now again teaching in a London school?'

He went on to enquire whether steps would be taken to ensure that teachers convicted of offences of this nature would not be allowed to teach British children. The question was clearly designed to embarrass Winston Churchill, as it was widely believed that, because of his friendship with Kath Duncan, he had seen to it that no charges would befall her husband. Kath Duncan, and certainly not Sandy, would never have abused or taken advantage of any friendship they had with the Churchills. Kath and Sandy fought their own battles and were quite prepared to take their punishment.

COPY OF MINUTE FROM THE GOVERNOR OF HOLLOWAY PRISON

DATED 29.12.32. re 6917 KATH DUNCAN.

2.

The Commissioners.

I beg to state that I received the above-named on the 19th instant on a Warrant in Default of Surety from Tower Bridge Police Court.

The writer of the letter, A. Duncan, has been he: to the Prison and in a very threatening tone has informed me that his wife is a Political prisoner and that she is entitled to the special privileges granted to some men who are at present in Brixton Prison.   He has already been informed that she is not entitled to any special privileg but I have made this woman a "Star" prisoner.

(Signed) J.H. MORTON.

In March, 1933, Lord Trenchard, the Commissioner of Police, placed a ban on all political meetings within 150 yards of labor exchanges – what we would call job centers today. These labor exchanges were key areas in which the Communist Party had been selling its papers and raising awareness of its campaigns, and where activists like Kath made speeches. Since the General Strike had been largely organized in this way, the authorities wanted to break this link by introducing the ban, and the police introduced automatic jail sentences for anyone who challenged it.

The Communist Party and the National Union of Unemployed Workers led the opposition to this new ban on the grounds that it was an encroachment on the freedom of speech and assembly, and Kath and Fred were the key speakers across London. The cause attracted thousands of people to the protests, and the ban was successfully broken at every single labor exchange, though a police report stated that N.U.W.M. had issued instructions to speakers to abstain from incitement of the audience that would result in a physical clash with police. Then, the campaign arrived in West Ham.

Initially, a crowd of several thousand had gathered to hear Fred speak, but this had dwindled to just a few hundred after a heavy downpour of rain. The police, having failed to stop them at every previous rally, charged the small crowd. After a brief scuffle, Fred found himself in the back of a police van and on the way to Plaistow Police Station. The charges, as always, were obstruction and the other 'crimes' they would usually charge unemployed activists with.

Kath and Sandy arrived at Plaistow at 3pm to put up bail for Fred. But the very next day, Fred Copeman, one of the Invergordon mutineers and the man who, just ten years later, would be rewarded with the OBE for services to his country, was sentenced to two months in Wormwood Scrubs. Prison was never a great deterrent for Fred, and he was later arrested in the same way at the East Ham Labour Exchange and was again sentenced to two months' prison, this time in Brixton Prison.

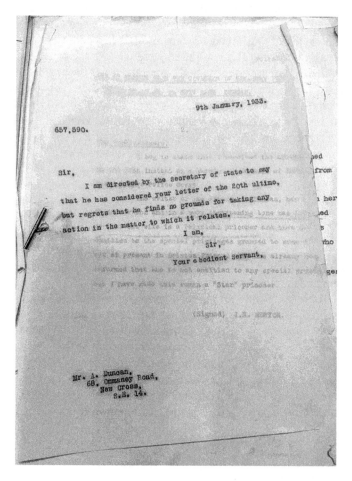

As always, Kath was at the prison gates to collect Fred and take him back to 68 Ommaney Road for a good breakfast. Mama was a great cook, and food was always on the stove, ready to feed the large number of people who would come and go throughout the day and often stay overnight at Kath and Sandy's warm and welcoming home.

The reports filed by spies at this period stated that the house was full of 'revolutionaries' and 'deviants', a standard way of referring to homosexuals and transvestite people. 68 Ommaney Road was not just a safe place where people could be who they wanted to be, amongst friends, but a place where they were encouraged and empowered to speak out and protest the ill treatment and injustice they suffered without fear.

The National Unemployed Workers' Movement was buoyed up after successfully taking the Commissioner of Police, Lord Trenchard, to court. He was the very man who had introduced the ban of workers protesting within 150 yards of labor exchanges. The N.U.W.M had argued and won their case that Lord Trenchard's officers had searched their offices and removed their documents without a search warrant. The counsel for the N.U.W.M were Sir Stafford Cripps, K.C., and D.N. Pritt, K.C. The court fined the police £50 and costs.

Fred and the Duncan household were beside themselves with delight. Fred Copeman later wrote about this, as follows: *'I was delighted to hear of this, for all three of my prison sentences had been received to force the breaking of Lord Trenchard's instructions, issued against what I considered to be the Common Law of the country. It was good that the courts upheld the position of the unemployed against the misuse of power by the Commissioner of Police.'* And thus, in an unprecedented ruling, the police had been found to have breached the law at a time when the word of any police officer would usually silence the voices of the many demanding free speech and civil rights, in all its forms.

A few days later, a large public meeting was organized. The meeting was open to all and focused on bringing the issue of the ban on assembly at labor exchanges to a head. Kath, as a leading member of the National Union of Unemployed Workers, would be their representative at the meeting, along with Fred Copeman. The unions, who were worried about the increasing threats from the government to its powerbase, also sent representatives to the meeting, as did the Council of Civil Liberties, which was just starting to find its feet and really needed a breakthrough case to raise its profile. It is still unclear as to why the Communist Party was not mentioned in the minutes of the meeting or why no party official was present, other than Kath, who by this time had been banned from holding office in the party.

At the meeting, it was decided that they would mount a definitive and large-scale challenge to the government's order banning activities outside labor exchanges by sending someone to stand up and speak at a large rally outside the labor exchange on Nynehead Street, in Deptford, in defiance of the ban. It was also agreed that everyone who had attended the meeting would be present to stand and witness in solidarity. But it had not been agreed who would be the principal in this action. Kath had listened closely to what everyone had had to say but needed to leave the meeting early, as she had to attend a public 'Friends of Russia' meeting in Woolwich, as she had been advertised as one of the speakers. She gave her excuses and went home to get ready.

When she arrived at home, Mama and some friends were reading the local papers and pointed out to Kath the report of the arrest and jailing of a good comrade who had been given a prison sentence simply for speaking out at an anti-fascist rally. When he had challenged the sentence as unjust, he had then been sentenced to hard labor.

In addition to this, two of her neighbors and closest gay friends, the journalist Henry Ward, 40-years-old, and his partner, Charles Thomas, 32-years-old, who lived on Brookmill Road, had been sentenced to 12 months' hard labor. In its reporting on the case, the *Kentish Mercury* quoted the chairman at Bromley Police Court as saying, 'You have a terrible record.' Mrs. A. G. Mann, passing sentence, placed Ward on remand for being a suspected person found loitering on Bromley Common, on 12 October, and with being a person admissible under the Prevention of Crimes Act; Thomas, a chauffeur, who lived at the same address as Ward, was sentenced to three months' imprisonment for being a suspected person found loitering at Bromley Common at the same time. 12 convictions, including 2 sentences of 3 years' penal servitude, were proved against Ward, and 5 convictions were proved against Thomas. It was stated that the men had met in prison.

Kath was incensed that Britain's prisons were increasingly being filled, not with murderers, burglars, and thieves, but ordinary workers, just because they were demanding fair wages and work conditions; the unemployed, just because they were looking for work; and gay people, just because they looked gay.

In the prevailing climate of massive police control and brutality, it seemed that the police could simply do or say what they liked, as the courts would never find against them. It seemed to Kath that the people had no say and no rights, and this was simply unacceptable. She could not expect the people she led to take direct action and face prison if she, as their leader, was not willing to do likewise. The arrest of her gay friends was the last straw and the trigger that made her miss her engagement in Woolwich – the only one she would ever miss – and rush back to the public meeting that was still going on at Greenwich community center to take responsibility for the latest campaign to secure civil rights for all.

Sandy was in mid-speech, talking about the injustice that everyone in the room had experienced. However, he made it clear that whoever took on the fight risked not only losing their jobs, but also incurring a stiff jail sentence and the devastating impact on their life, which was certain to follow. "How could anyone in the room," he asked, "expect our Kath to put herself through it? Had she not done more than any other for the cause, and for the nation at large, through a lifetime of activism? Why, whenever there is a call to arms, whether it be to do with Deptford Market, slum landlords, the arms trade, welfare reform, women's rights, or gay rights, is it always my Kath, our Kath, who leads the way? Was it not time that others there put themselves forward?"

The room fell silent as everyone gradually became aware that Kath had unexpectedly returned to the meeting and was at the back of the hall. As Sandy finished, Kath walked to the front and spoke:

"No woman could want for a finer husband and comrade. I have just listened to all that you have said and gone away and reflected, but I cannot, as a woman, as an activist, as a communist, continue to ask my fellow comrades to keep fighting our battles if, when the big battle comes, as now, I shy away. I have loved teaching my children with a passion. I have loved marching and singing The Internationale with every one of you in this room. But free speech, the right to protest, must be a basic human right. The right for every one of us to choose whom we love should not be a decision for the courts. We have just fought a world war; do not we all deserve better? I will go to Nynehead Street, and I will do what we need to do."

A member of the committee pointed out that this would be difficult, because spies were everywhere, and if the authorities knew what the activists were doing, they would do their best not to arrest anyone, for fear of creating martyrs. Kath reminded everyone, "Comrades, we have spies everywhere, and occasionally, I am told, even in my home. When should we do this?"

The meeting agreed the date and time for the action, and everyone on the committee agreed to attend. Kath pledged to 'chalk up' around Deptford to maximize the numbers who would attend. The protest was on.

Kath was being watched almost night and day, making it increasingly hard for her to go about her activism and chalk up – using chalk to write slogans and graffiti. Kath would never allow her situation or her activism to be tempered in any way, and being as spirited as she was, it was not long before she discovered a fresh way to outsmart the spies in the street outside her home. With the help of Mama and Sandy, Kath put on Sandy's clothes, covered her hair in one of Sandy's hats, and got him to lower her out of the rear bedroom window with Mama holding onto Sandy's ankles. It was 2am when she climbed over the fence of her rear garden to make her way to Nynehead Street. While many of the activists who chalked up were caught, fined, or jailed, Kath never was. On this occasion, she chalked across the whole of Nynehead Street this legend:

'SEDITION
Meeting at the Test Centre today (Now) 1pm

Speakers: R. Kidd (Council for Civil Liberties).
A.M. Bing (Barrister-At-Law).
E. Hanley (Amalgamated Engineers Union).
K. Duncan (National Unemployed Workers Movement).
Defend the right of free speech and public meeting.'

Kath then rushed back home and pulled on the knotted rope that was hanging from her bedroom window and tied to Sandy's arm, in case he fell asleep or did not hear her whistle, and went to bed.

By 1pm, a large crowd had gathered at the Training Centre on Nynehead Street, Deptford, in defiance of the ban. Kath's famous soapbox stage, which enabled her small figure to be clearly seen by the large crowd, had been placed in the roadway opposite the entrance to the Training Centre. Kath was about to stand on it, when the chief constable of the district, together with William Jones, an inspector of the Metropolitan Police, proceeded to tell everyone that this meeting was in breach of the regulations and could not be held in Nynehead Street, but could be held on Desmond Street, 175 yards away.

As the main point of the protest was the restriction of where protests could and could not be held, the offer of Desmond Street was simply not an option for Kath and her comrades. And so, as she was helped up onto her box to speak, saying, "I'm going to hold it!" she was arrested and taken into custody.

On 6 August, 1934, on her first appearance at Tower Bridge Police Court, she was able to have the case set aside for seven days to enable her to secure the legal defense that the now renamed National Council of Civil Liberties would supply. Still feared by the state as a radical revolutionary, she was tailed by operatives of MI5, who reported that, after she left court, she was met by her husband, Ronald Kidd, and Ken Harvey. 'Ronald Kidd, after a short consultation with Duncan, drove away in a motor car, index number: Y.M.8389. The Duncans and Harvey took refreshments at a local public house and then departed by tram to Greenwich. No attempt was made to demonstrate outside the police court, where not more than 12 persons were assembled.'

The notes of Police Sergeant William East clearly show that the police case put before the judge in both of Kath's trials was based on lies and, had the judges been made aware of the contents of the secret MI5 reports on Kath's activities, they would probably not have been able to convict her.

Kath Duncan was charged under the Prevention of Crimes Act 1871, S.12, as amended by the Prevention of Crimes Amendment Act 1885, S.A. It was alleged that, on 30 July, 1934, Kath 'did unlawfully and willfully obstruct the respondent when in the execution of his duty.' Kath's defense was that she had not obstructed either the highway or the Training Centre; the only obstruction she admitted to was her box being placed on the roadway and the people surrounding it. It was stressed that neither the appellant nor any of the persons present at the meeting had committed, incited, or provoked any breach of the peace. The magistrate was not persuaded and found Kath guilty as charged, who then found herself, in December, 1934, spending a second wedding anniversary in Holloway Prison.

Conditions in the prison were very poor, and Kath's health was seriously compromised; she contracted tuberculosis and this disease would see to it that the oppressed poor would be deprived of Kath's tireless activism far too early.

The prison governor was shocked that Kath had been jailed for 12 months, a sentence which, in his view, would only turn her into a martyr. With her establishment connections, Kath was more than, in his words, a 'star' prisoner, as she was the subject of the first parliamentary debate on civil rights in British history, led by George Lansbury, the leader of the Labour Party. The Scot from Deptford might have been in a jail cell in Holloway, but her activism was front-page news across the world. The stand she had taken and the sentence she had received would permanently change the conception of civil rights and the way in which protests were managed and policed. This crucial debate in the House of Commons, as published in *Hansard*, is reprinted in full as the next chapter, so as to enable the reader to form an idea of the broader issues Kath's campaign for civil rights engaged with, and how her activities led to the establishment of the National Council of Civil Liberties, which is simply known as Liberty today.

Kath's second term in jail would be very different from her first. Demonstrations were held almost every day, and there was a relentless stream of letters calling for her release. The court had jailed her, and she could only do as the law dictated. But this time, Kath had Her Majesty's Opposition, as well as senior members of the government, on her side. Although just about every radical and political activist in the land were now marching behind Kath Duncan's flag, and many unions and women's groups wrote letters and organized protests demanding her release, there is no record of any letters being sent by the Communist Party or any record of any demonstrations organized by the Party in support of Kath.

Again, her sentence was mysteriously and dramatically reduced from 12 months to one month. After serving this reduced term, which she spent sewing shirts she would later declare no one would ever find fit to wear, she was met upon her release by a large delegation of women and escorted to a rally on her beloved Deptford Broadway. A 'welcome home' party was held at Greenwich Baths.

A few days after her warm welcome back in Deptford, Kath received a letter from her employer, the London County Council Education Committee, saying that they would be removing her name from the list of approved teachers. A campaign was immediately launched to overturn the decision and 5,700 signed a petition in support of Kath. There were two testimonials from head teachers, resolutions of protests from local trades unions, and legal support from her union, the National Union of Teachers. Soon enough, the *South London* again published what would become a regular headline: 'KATH DUNCAN WINS!'

Kath, reinstated as a teacher, threw herself even more whole-heartedly into her activism to repay her supporters for the show of solidarity that had helped and supported her yet again.

She spoke in support of the all-London bus strike and also raised awareness of Gandhi and his cause, and of the heavy sentences being given to union members in India. She joined forces with the activist Wal Hannington, who, like her, had also been found guilty of sedition and had just been released from jail after a three-month term. She also called for the police to join the working-class movement to fight their own 10% wage cut. In February, Kath was one of the keynote speakers at the national T.U.C. rally in Hyde Park. The political climate was changing: the police-state mentality was slowly being rolled back, and the civil rights that Kath had fought so long and hard for were coming of age.

In 1933, the Reichstag building in Berlin was burning as
the Nazis sought to proclaim themselves as the only possible
saviors of Germany.

Kath, who, some years before, had done so much to fight
fascism and had played a key role in the Cable Street protests,
now spoke out in Deptford against the rise of Hitler in
Germany. She said that the burning of the German parliament
building was a symbol of the Nazi determination to destroy
democracy. She would then ask the crowds: 'Would the British

capitalist class be any less callous to the unemployed? Would they hesitate to use fascism in Britain?'

The banner of the National Union Workers Movement proclaimed: 'Forward to the Fight against Hunger and Fascism!' Kath would march with that banner many times and would always make sure that any fascist chants or speeches were drowned out by the sound of her and her comrades singing *The Red Flag* as loudly as they could.

Chapter Six
National Unemployed Workers'
Movement (Arrests)

HC Deb, 22 December, 1932, vol 273 cc1268–300

George Lansbury – Leader of the Labour Party: There are two reasons why this debate, as I understand, could not usefully be carried further today. One is that the Right Hon. Gentleman himself has to attend a meeting of the Round Table Conference this afternoon, and also, we on this side want to raise a domestic question, and there are other members who desire to raise other domestic questions. He will allow me to say on the question of the papers that I am obliged to him for his courtesy in offering to show me the paper he thinks I refer to, but before settling my mind on the subject, I should prefer to look at the OFFICIAL REPORT, because I think that – perhaps it is from my side – we are misunderstanding each other as to the particular paper to which I refer. The only other thing I want to say is that I hope the Right Hon. Gentleman, when he comes to consider the question of goodwill and an amnesty in India, will keep in mind the fact that his position is that of representing authority which has really impressed itself – if his statement is correct – upon the mass of opinion in India, and that if there is any giving way to be done, it should be done by the strongest side. Most of the leaders who are in prison are personal friends of mine, and I think many of them are personal friends of many other members in this House and in another place. Very nearly a year has passed since Gandhi was put into prison, with a number of others, and he has been kept there waiting for pledges. I do not think pledges to be extracted from people under those conditions are much use.

1269 I ask the Right Hon. Gentleman to remember that if Mr. Gandhi died tomorrow, every kind of tribute would be paid to him by opponents as well as by friends. I ask him to consider between now and Sunday whether it would not be worthwhile, seeing the conditions prevailing in India today, to make a big gesture, to have a gaol delivery and free these men on their own sort of responsibility. If what he said is true – and of course we accept the Right Hon. Gentleman's statement about the provincial assemblies and the general spirit of goodwill – why not add to that goodwill by setting this man and his friends free? The Right Hon. Gentleman will agree that no one accuses him of anything but the most honorable and patriotic intentions towards his own people. Having said that, I will just leave the matter there and hope the Right Hon. Gentleman will give our appeal his best consideration.

The subject that I want to bring before the House is that of the case of Mr. Tom Mann and the other persons who are at present detained because they refused to give sureties. Mrs. Duncan was also charged in Southeast London, as well as Tom Mann and his friends. I hope that the Home Secretary will consider this matter very carefully. We are of the opinion that, during the last few years – I raised this question when the Right Hon. Gentleman, the member for Darwen (Sir H. Samuel), was Home Secretary – that the police authorities generally and the Metropolitan Police especially have taken up an attitude towards public meetings and processions which is, relatively speaking, new.

The start of these restrictions took place during the Home Rule discussion and during the unemployment meetings after 1886. Anyone who is acquainted with the history of public meetings in London knows that until 1886, there never was any question of note-takers at open-air meetings or of police note-takers at indoor meetings. I am sorry that there is no representative here of the Liberal Party, because the Liberal Party and the Home Rulers who were in this House at the time raised the question and brought before the House the new position that had arisen. I called attention to it because I thought that it was the beginning of spying upon political opponents. Those who raised the question at that time said that they did so because it was the sort of thing that was bound to grow. The practice has grown. Until today, the most innocent meetings in London are subject to it. If you look round in those meetings, you will find someone there representing Scotland Yard, as if it were the business of Scotland Yard to know what people's political opinions are. We used to think that that kind of thing only happened in despotic countries.

I repeat that, in London, this sort of thing only started after 1886. I am quite certain that Conservative meetings, official Liberal meetings, and official Labour meetings are not dealt with in this fashion. It is only what are considered to be, in the police's judgment, if you please, a sort of outside or left-wing or communist meeting that is so dealt with. It is no business of the police to know what any of the citizens are thinking about or what they are talking about. The present home secretary and other home secretaries have again and again, in answer to questions, said that the advocacy of communism is not an offence against the law. What do the police want to attend communist meetings for, or have spies at communist meetings, or at Independent Labour Party meetings, or at meetings of the Socialist League for? What is it to do with them? Let them mind their own business and look after burglars and people of that kind. It is not their right to know what a man is speaking about or what theory is being advocated.

M.P. TO ASK
ABOUT
A TEACHER

SENTENCED — BUT SHE IS KEEPING HER JOB

"INCITEMENT"

A QUESTION about a woman school teacher who has served a term of one month's imprisonment for incitement in a public speech is to be asked in Parliament next week by Captain A. L. S. Todd.

He will ask the Minister of Education whether he is aware that Mrs. K. Duncan, an L.C.C. teacher, was only cautioned by the L.C.C. education committee following her sentence, and is now again teaching in a London school, and whether steps will be taken to ensure that teachers convicted of offences of this nature are not allowed to teach British children.

Mrs. Duncan was called on at Tower Bridge Police Court in December last to find a surety of £50 to be of good behaviour. She refused, and was sent to prison for a month in default.

She was accused, under a statute of Edward III., of making a speech calculated to cause a breach of the peace at a meeting of the National Unemployed Workers' Movement at Bermondsey.

It may be said, 'Oh yes, but we do not go there for that purpose; we go there for the purpose of hearing whether people are saying anything seditious.' I have been a victim of these gentlemen who go to inquire as to what we say at meetings. The late Lord Brentford read a statement late one night of something that I was alleged to have said. After the adjournment, because there was no time to discuss the matter before, he was good enough to show me the document. Everybody who knows me knows that I never said anything of the kind. The gentleman who took the note must have written it out of his imagination, because if there is one thing that my worst opponent, either Communist or Tory, will not charge me with, it is the advocacy of violence. I am known as a person who gets shouted down at meetings because I denounce violence, and yet here is a police officer giving information which put into my mouth words that I had never uttered. I am sure that the gentleman who did it wrote it in longhand and had no knowledge of shorthand. It would be interesting to know how many of these note-takers are expert shorthand writers. Everyone knows that reporting is a very skilled business. You can miss a word or you can put a word in.

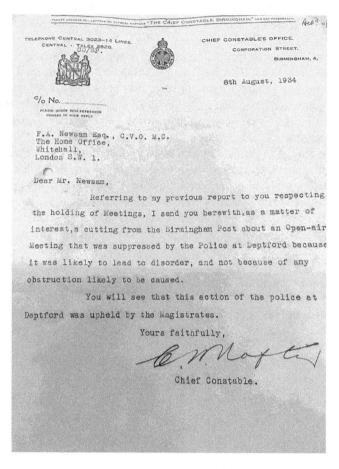

TELEPHONE CENTRAL 3023-14 LINES.
CENTRAL - TELEX 2626.
00/SP.

CHIEF CONSTABLE'S OFFICE.
CORPORATION STREET.
BIRMINGHAM, 4.

8th August, 1934

C/o No.

PLEASE QUOTE THIS REFERENCE
NUMBER IN YOUR REPLY

F.A. Newsam Esq., C.V.O. M.C.
The Home Office,
Whitehall,
London S.W. 1.

Dear Mr. Newsam,

Referring to my previous report to you respecting the holding of Meetings, I send you herewith, as a matter of interest, a cutting from the Birmingham Post about an Open-air Meeting that was suppressed by the Police at Deptford because it was likely to lead to disorder, and not because of any obstruction likely to be caused.

You will see that this action of the police at Deptford was upheld by the Magistrates.

Yours faithfully,

Chief Constable.

The police authorities in London have been permitted to arrogate to themselves the right to go about and discover when meetings are being held and who is going to conduct them. I attended one meeting, and the police came – this was a year or two back, but it is being done now – and they wanted a list of people who were going to speak. I raised a question in the House, and I was told that no one had instructed them but that they wanted to know. I expect that there was a burglary going on around the corner, or perhaps a murder, but instead of the police attending to their own business, they were interfering with something that was absolutely no concern of theirs.

Then, there is the growth of what we consider as militarism in the police. I have raised this question before, and no one yet has answered it. I raise it again today, and I hope that the Right Hon. Gentleman, the Home Secretary, will give me an answer. In 1886, when there were disturbances, and in the year or two that followed, you could not have had a charge of the police or of the military as you can today. You could not have the sort of charge by the police that you have nowadays, when they plunge into a crowd on horseback armed with long sticks. That never happened. When there was danger of a riot, the Riot Act was read, and the people were warned to disperse. There is no warning today. I am speaking of what I know. No one rides along and says to the people on the pavement, 'You must clear off,' but they just gallop along and charge into the people. I have been ridden down myself when walking along Roman Road, at Bow, by patrols on the pavement, and no notice was given that we were doing anything – in fact, we were not doing anything – illegal. We were just charged by the police.

I want to know why it is that the authorities have taken this power. They apparently have the power because they do not use firearms. You may not fire on the people, but you can injure the people just as much by riding them down with horses. Some of the stories that are told about what happened in Hyde Park on that particular Sunday, and about what happened during the disturbances outside this House in October, go to show that the police today imagine that they have the right to disperse a crowd anyhow. If you compare the manner in which they disperse a Labour or Socialist crowd with their manner of dealing with a crowd which assembles to see a great wedding outside the Abbey or St. Margaret's, and which is equally a nuisance, there is a great difference. It does not matter that there is inconvenience to the general public who want to go about their business, that the road is blocked and people have to go round, and so on; the treatment is altogether different.

We feel that the police authorities in London, under the control of military people, of people who are accustomed to order people about, have got it into their heads that they are the masters of this city; but they are no more the masters than anyone else, and they have no right to do anything in the way of ordering the citizens hither and thither just as they please.

Certainly, no set of people has the right to ride down the general public without having given any notice whatsoever that they are called upon to disperse. Not so long ago, a justice of the peace had to be present to read the proclamation calling upon the citizens to disperse, but under this military autocracy in London, power has been taken to deal with the public in an altogether different manner. The Communist Party and ourselves have nothing in common so far as tactics are concerned. We shall denounce any attempt to incite people to violence under any sort of conditions. That is a matter about which we are denounced by the Communist Party, and it is not in defense of this order that we are raising the question today. It is because official appetites grow with what they feed on. It is the Communists today; it may be ourselves tomorrow. We say that because there is no sort of equality of treatment in this matter.

I should like to draw the attention of the House to the fact that there is a fascist organization in London today, which makes much more seditious speeches than are made by any communist in the country. But no one takes any notice of them; no one has yet attempted to stop the drilling of the fascists.

The example, to which I will call attention later, of Lord Carson's agitation in Ireland, is being followed in London. During one of my elections – I think it was the election before last – a set of able-bodied, well-fed, well-groomed, well-to-do young men marched through my division for the purpose, if you please, of preserving order. I took no notice of them, because the women took them in hand and smacked their faces for them. But I am perfectly certain that, if they had been 20 or 30 communists, in red shirts instead of black shirts, who had gone into a Tory constituency, the police would have dealt with them. This matter, really, is entirely a class business. The Blackshirts in London are being organized, and they may make their speeches. I notice that Hon. Gentlemen smile, but one of these days, when Mosley marches up here, they will, perhaps, smile the other way.

I come to another fact. In dealing with these particular cases, so far as I can understand, the Right Hon. Gentleman and those who advised the prosecution have not prosecuted for anything that has been done, or anything that has been said;

they only anticipated that something might be said or something might be done. Before I proceed to that subject, however, I should like to say a word about Tom Mann. I have no personal knowledge of either of the two other prisoners, but Tom Mann is my friend. I have known him practically all his life, and I know him as a man who is rather different from the ordinary agitator. He has not, from agitation, become a member of Parliament, and from a member of Parliament a member of the government; he has remained an agitator all his life. I do not think that that is any discredit to him; I think it is greatly to his credit.

I have never known him – the Right Hon. Gentleman and his advisers might look up their records – I have never known him to advocate violence. I have never known him to advocate that unarmed men should go against armed men. He may have done what Sir Oswald Mosley is doing now, that is to say, talked about the day when the workers would probably have to fight for their rights; but I never remember him urging men to throw themselves against the police or the military. In any case, what has he done all his life? What has been his job in life? He has simply been working for poor people, and his position today is that he is a very poor man indeed, so that no one in this House can stand up and charge him with being 'on the make'. That may be done with people like me; it has been done sometimes – [Hon. Members: "Hear, hear!"] Those of you who are not 'on the make', look in a looking-glass. The fact is that he is a very poor man, and he is a poor man not because he has not brains enough to be a rich man, but because he chose to give his life in that particular way to the people to whom he belongs. Therefore, I think he is entitled to some consideration at the hands of this House and of the Ministry.

There are one or two things that he has not done, and this brings me to another matter on which the Solicitor-General may have something to say, if he is going to speak. Tom Mann has never yet led a riot at a church, such as has taken place at St. Hilary, in Cornwall, within the last few weeks. Apparently, the Solicitor-General does not know anything about that case. They were only Protestant agitators; the Solicitor-General only knows about communist agitators. The police do not trouble about such people, which shows that there is only one particular set of law breakers in this connection that they know anything about. It has been referred to in all the newspapers, and I do not understand the Hon. and Learned Gentleman not knowing anything about it. Why did he not prosecute them? Everyone knows when people are told that they are to assemble and prevent Mass from being said – I am not talking about moving the ornaments, but about what happened within the last three weeks, when, during a service, the people were incited to go.

Frank Boyd Merriman – first and last Baron Merriman and a Manchester MP: The Right Hon. Gentleman has raised this topic and has challenged me. Will he permit me to say, first of all, that the police were present, and secondly, that they are prosecuting?

George Lansbury: Yes, but you took no steps to prevent the disturbance taking place. One would have thought, when you were going to have a disturbance in the church, you would have used these powers that you are using against Tom Mann to prevent the scandal and the outrage taking place. You have not the pluck to do that, because they have very powerful friends, and you only attack those who cannot hit you back. Tom Mann has not organized a volunteer army yet; he has not imported arms into the country, and he has not yet started drilling, as do the fascists. I intended to refer to the Elias case, but I understand that there is an appeal and that I must not touch it.

Let me come to the case of Mrs. Kate Duncan. I am going to speak now with very great deference in the presence of my Hon. and Learned Friend, and of the Solicitor-General, because I suppose this is very much a matter of law. This woman was a disturber of the peace and an inciter of others to commit crime, and, as such, subject to the provisions of the Statute of 34 Edward III. What is this statute? I was a victim of it. You may have this lady in the House, as well as myself one of these days, and, having been prosecuted, she may even speak from this box. Here is the sort of thing that this act was passed to deal with.

Last year, this same public department had great trouble in dealing with the opening of cinemas and such places on Sunday because of a silly old law, and everyone stood up and said, 'These laws ought to be swept away.' Of all the tomfool laws to apply in modern times, this one takes the biscuit. That in every county of England shall be assigned for the keeping of the peace, one lord, and with him three or four of the most worthy in the county, with some learned in the law, and they shall have power to restrain the offenders, rioters, and all other barraters and to pursue, arrest, take, and chastise them according to their trespass or offence. Of course, now you are not allowed to chastise them. I should like to see you start chastising them. It means that you can flog them before you imprison them; and to cause them to be imprisoned and duly punished, according to the law and customs of the realm. There is no law and custom now to allow the police to chastise anyone.

Knight: It is all obsolete.

Lansbury: This is the act under which they are put away.

Knight: A historical document.

Lansbury: Member will restrain his impatience and allow me to read it so that the House can decide. According to the law and customs of the realm, and according to that which to them shall seem best to do and good advisement; and also to inform them.

It reads like a novel, and an ancient one at that – '*and to inquire of all those that have been pillors and robbers in the parts beyond the sea.*' Is it charged against Tom Mann and Mrs. Duncan that they are robbers across the sea? '*And be now come again and go wandering*' – Tom Mann has a residence. He does not wander. He is not a vagrant. '*And will not labor.*' There is no charge against him that he will not labor. He is six years older than the old age pension age. He has committed no crime, and even if he had he does not work, as they were wont in times past, no one accuses him of not having worked. He was an engineer – and to take and arrest all those that they may find by indictment, or by suspicion, and to put them in prison; and to take of all them that be of good fame.

There was a great controversy about the word 'not' which has been interpolated here when I was before the court. The judges decided that it did not matter whether the act of Parliament had been altered or not. They said, 'This chap has to be put away and put away he must be.' When you come to interpret the law, you lawyers are wonderful people, especially when you become judges. You really make law. A very learned counsel, Mr. Montague Shearman, argued that this word 'not', having been interpolated into the Norman French, which I cannot read, really vitiated the law, so far as I was concerned. The judges said, 'No one took much notice of it in the past, and we are not going to take any notice of it today,' so I went down.

It reads without the interpolation. '*And to take of all them that be of good fame.*' That is not very good sense, so some Johnny put in 'not' in order to make sense of it. He said, 'This is what they meant, and I will make the law read what they meant instead of what they said.' I do not think that is good enough. '*Nor put in the peril which may happen of such offenders: And also to hear and determine at the King's suit all manner of felonies and trespasses done in the same county according to the laws and customs aforesaid.*' I do not think I need read any more. I suggest that this would be good bedtime reading for anyone who really wants to see the kind of law under which communists and other people are dealt with. You only deal with communists and common people under this law. You dare not bring it into operation against the Kensitites, the Mosleyites, or Carson and company. No one can deny that. It is only poor people.

Mrs. Kate Duncan was charged. Let us see the evidence that she was a killer, a robber, a wanderer, and a vagabond, and that she had done something she ought not to have done. The Right Hon. Gentleman may have a longer report of the case. I am only able to quote from the report in the *Times*. Mr. Clayton, the solicitor, said that, in a speech in Bermondsey Town Hall, this lady spoke in a manner calculated to create a breach of the peace, that the defendant seemed – not that she had – to have taken a very prominent part, and that she repeated these words at subsequent meetings as well: 'The Public Assistance people should be held personally responsible.' I have said that myself many a time and have never been proceeded against. Then, Mr. Clayton gives evidence. He is a solicitor. He makes a statement. Mr. Clayton said that he thought that Duncan was then speaking about a Bermondsey murder case. What right has he to pretend to say what he thought. What a solicitor thinks is not evidence, however distinguished he may be. He says that 'he thinks' that she was referring to a Bermondsey murder case.

The Public Assistance people should be identified and their addresses found in order that pressure can be brought to bear upon them. Pressure is brought to bear upon me every day. Numbers of people come to my house when I am at home, asking me and begging of me to bring pressure to bear upon this House and upon other people, and, no doubt, bringing pressure to bear upon me to do my job. And why should they not?

George Buchanan – Glasgow Labour MP: What about the tariff people?

Lansbury: The tariff people come here. She says that it is the duty of the workers to do this. Is that wrong? What is there in that? Every member of a local Public Assistance committee who refuses relief to unemployed men or who wants to send an unemployed man to Belmont must be identified so that he can be intimidated. [An Hon. Member: 'Hear, hear.']

Wait a minute. Mr. Clayton said that the director considered that those words were calculated to provoke a breach of the peace, and that there was no doubt that Duncan had personally endeavored to carry out those threats. But wait a minute. The fact that the solicitor said that is not evidence that the woman said it. It was much too previous. Detective Inspector Jones, of the Special Branch, said that he was at the meeting in question and heard Duncan use the words alleged. He did not take a shorthand note. He made a note soon afterwards. There is an outrage. That proves exactly what I was saying about myself. I feel strongly about this matter, because, as I have said, the late Lord Brentford stood up in this House and said that he had a note of something which I had said at Poplar Town Hall, and I had said nothing of the kind. There never had been a shorthand note taken. It was a longhand note written afterwards. This man was honest enough to say that he wrote down afterwards what he thought the woman had said.

Then, the magistrate lends a hand in the giving of the evidence, and I call attention to this fact. The magistrate said: "I see that you have been merciful to this woman." He looked at the officer's notebook and said: "Besides, what you have given in evidence," what he had remembered, but not what he had written down at the time, "I see you have got in your note 'These people are not necessarily local and can walk about under the Common Law without being hissed, booed, or spat upon by the workers.'" The workers are very peaceful and law-abiding, and, if she said it, it only means that she told them what, apparently, everybody knew.

Then, Detective Phillips said that he saw Duncan at a demonstration in Hollydale Road, Peckham, outside the works of Mr. Evan Cooke, a borough councilor: 'The demonstrators – not this woman – used filthy and insulting words.' They then went to Camberwell Town Hall, where they were refused admission. Meetings have been held outside my house and most uncomplimentary things have been said about me by tariff reformers. [An Hon. Member: 'Hear, hear.'] Oh, yes, I have had men outside my door calling me everything from a pickpocket to the Lord-knows-what. Do you think that I care? It does not make any difference to me at all. But I would not dream of asking that somebody should be locked up because he was intimidating me. The point is that there is not a scrap of evidence that the woman used any of this filthy language. The Right Hon. Gentleman has perhaps a longer note of it than I have, but in the report in the *Times,* there is not a word of evidence that this woman used this language at all. This is how the press reports a poor woman. I have read this sort of thing about myself, and therefore, I repeat that I feel very keenly about it.

Duncan, in a long, rambling speech, denied that she had used any insulting words or conduct likely to provoke a breach of the peace. She had been a public worker for five years and would not do anything so foolish. There is not a scrap of definite evidence against the woman. She gives her own version of the case, and she has as much right to be listened to as those people who did not write down but merely remembered. Mr. Campion, the magistrate, said that he would be willing to take Duncan's word. That shows the impression which the woman and the evidence had made upon the magistrate. He said that he would take her word that no such conduct would happen again and would bind her over in her own recognizances to keep the peace for six months. Mrs. Duncan said, "What if I refuse?" And Mr. Campion said, "You will have to find a surety of £50." Mrs. Duncan: "I do not want any surety." I want to say on that point, that when I was before the magistrates, I could have gone free by finding sureties, but I would not find sureties and pledge myself to do something which I had no intention of doing. I considered it a gross insult and denial of justice to ask me to give such pledge. This woman was in the same position. I call the attention of the Home Secretary to the fact that the magistrate was willing to let her off on her word without any sureties at all, unless this report is wrong. I will read it again: 'He would be willing to take Duncan's word that no such conduct would happen again.'

Oliver Stanley – Tory MP, Bristol: Read the next few words.

Lansbury: All right. 'That no such conduct would happen again.'

Stanley: The next few words.

Lansbury: And would bind her over in her own recognizances to keep the peace for six months. That meant herself. She said: 'What if I refuse?' The magistrate replied: 'Then I shall want you to find a surety.' When she refused to find sureties, she was ordered to go to prison for a month in default. According to the magistrate's own statement, he was willing to take the woman's word in the matter. That being so, it must have been in his mind that there was some doubt as to whether she was the kind of woman stated by the prosecution. Unless the Right Hon. Gentleman has some evidence which is not given in the report in the *Times*, I say that there is no evidence against the woman. It is not worth the paper that it is written on. I should like the Home Secretary or the Solicitor-General to give us some reason why the woman cannot be released forthwith and allowed to go free.

When we come to the case of Tom Mann and his friend, it is a little complicated, because of the Act of 1817. Here is what Mr. Wallace said for the prosecution: he would ask that the accused men be ordered to enter into their own recognizances and to find surety, or sureties, for their future good behavior and to keep the peace. The court had power to make such an order under a very old act, the Act of Edward III, and the Seditious Meetings Act, 1817, which said that meetings of more than 50 persons within a mile of Westminster – during the sitting of Parliament or of the Superior Courts, for the purpose or on the pretext of considering or preferring a petition, complaint, remonstrance, or address to the King, or either House of Parliament, for alterations in matters of Church or state – were deemed to be unlawful assemblies. I would point out that part of that act is already obsolete. The Courts of Justice were formerly alongside Westminster Hall and were part of this building. Now, they are situated in the Strand, and any procession at any time can go past the law courts. I came past the law courts with a great procession when the Poplar councilors were tried. We were escorted through the city of London and treated quite properly by the authorities. We marched right up to the courts. Nobody thinks now of stopping a procession simply because it is passing the law courts, but this act says that you must not take a procession past the law courts.

I am advised that unlawful assembly – I hope the Home Secretary will pay attention to this point – does not constitute a breach of the peace. Therefore, whatever the charge was against these men, it could not be a charge concerning a breach of the peace. Unlawful assembly is mentioned in the Act of 1817. Therefore, the Right Hon. Gentleman must prove something more than was proven at the court.

Mr. Wallace went on to say: 'The accused men were well-known members of the Communist Party.' It is a matter of agreement between us that to be a member of the Communist Party is not something illegal. I should, however, like to ask the Home Secretary a question on that point, so that that position may be affirmed. Membership of the Communist Party or of the National Committee of the Unemployed is not illegal. They have not been proclaimed illegal organizations. We have not come to that yet. Therefore, there is nothing against the men because they are members of the Communist party.

The statement proceeds were two of the four national officials of the National Unemployed Workers' Movement. That is not illegal. That is no crime either against the common law or against any particular law. In the 5th December issue of the *Daily Worker*, the organ of the Communist Party, there was an article which began: '*Unemployed! Call For Action on 20th December. Fight for petition to be presented to Parliament.*' I have written that sort of thing many times. So has the Right Hon. Gentleman, when he has asked the electors to fight for tariff reform and the Conservative Party. It does not necessarily mean that you are going to fight in any other sense than we fight one another across this piece of oak furniture, or whatever furniture it is.

'Appeal to trade unionists.' 'Starvation is attacking every working-class home.' Is anyone going to say that that is an illegal statement? It may be an illegal statement in the minds of the Metropolitan Police officials, who are now all military gentlemen and want to use the British public as if they were private soldiers in their charge. We are facing the blackest winter in history, with the national government launching more vicious economies and reducing the working classes to slave conditions. Is there anything illegal in that statement? Will the Right Hon. Gentleman tell us what there is criminal in these statements?

The call to action calls for mass action to secure winter and Christmas relief, abolition of the means test, and for the right of hunger marchers to present the means test petition to Parliament. What is there illegal or unlawful in that? The Right Hon. Gentleman has to prove that these men were guilty of inciting people to do something that was unlawful. They have done nothing of the kind. There is nothing in that article which incites anybody to do anything that is illegal, and the Right Hon. Gentleman knows that as well as I do. There is not a scrap of evidence to show that Tom Mann or Llewellyn ever wrote that article or were employed on the *Daily Worker*. There is not a scrap of evidence that they had any connection whatsoever with it. You might as well say that I am responsible for what appears in the *Daily Herald* because I am a member of a party...

Buchanan: They are bad enough, but they would not go to that length.

Lansbury: I subscribe to the people who represent the Labour movement on the board of the *Daily Herald*. Suppose the *Daily Herald* libeled somebody. I should not be personally responsible for that any more than the noble lord, the Member for Southampton, (Lord Apsley) is responsible for the *Morning Post*. I believe he is a director, or was a director, of the *Morning Post*, but he was never responsible and could not be responsible for the editor. Because Tom Mann is a member of the Communist Party, he cannot be held responsible for what every writer in the *Daily Worker* writes. When I edited the *Daily Herald*, I had to be responsible for what others wrote, and I was never allowed to shirk my responsibility. I was editor.

Tom Mann is not the editor of the *Daily Worker*, and as far as the evidence goes, there is not a scrap to show that he had anything to do with the *Daily Worker*. There is no evidence that he or Llewellyn wrote the article or had anything to do with it. I hope the Right Hon. Gentleman will not ride off on this matter, because this is really the gravamen of the case. There is nothing else against them, except that in some way they are linked up with this article in the *Daily Worker*. I challenge the Right Hon. Gentleman to prove any connection other than that they were members of the Communist Party, and that they were officials of the National Unemployed Workers' Society.

On 9th December, a letter headed '*The National Unemployed Workers' Movement, the National Administrative Council*' – those are not very revolutionary words – was delivered to the Prime Minister at the House of Commons. It described the officials as Mr. Elias, Mr. Wal Hannington as the organizer, Mr. Tom Mann as the treasurer, and Mr. Llewellyn as the secretary. The letter was as follows: 'Following our request prior to Tuesday, 1st November, to you and the Speaker of the House to allow a deputation of the unemployed and employed representatives to present a petition to which we have one million signatures, and also to allow this representative delegation to state their views before the House. We are going to make a similar request that you meet this deputation on 19th December. The deputation will also present the million signatures petition. It is our opinion that the government, and particularly yourself as responsible head of the government, should have regard to the views of over one million people in this country who have signed this national petition, which we desire to present and await your reply to this request.' What is there illegal in that? I should have thought it was a respectable, courteous, and gentlemanly letter, written in the best Oxford and Cambridge style. I want someone to tell me any particular sentence in this letter which is illegal.

Mr. Wallace, in his submission, said that the letter clearly connected the National Unemployed Workers' Movement with the publication in the *Daily Worker*, and that the people responsible were Mann and Llewellyn. Is there a shred of evidence of any connection between the two? I have read what the *Daily Worker* said. They called for mass action, a gathering of the unemployed, not specifying where, and this letter was written asking the Prime Minister to receive a deputation.

In 1922, I remember that I raised the question as to the then Prime Minister, Mr. Bonar Law, receiving a similar deputation. I went to Downing Street and saw Mr. Bonar Law. He met the deputation and prevented a great deal of trouble. The Right Hon. Member for Carnarvon Boroughs (Mr. Lloyd George), under much more difficult circumstances, received a very big deputation in Downing Street, and it is a pity that succeeding governments have broken with that procedure.

The representatives of people who are suffering as the unemployed ought to be heard. I am not arguing as to whether these people are the best or the worst representatives; that is not the point. They represent, however, a considerable feeling in this country, and they have a petition which they say is signed by one million persons. They have a right to bring that petition to the House and to ask for permission to present it, although the House can deny them the right to come to the Bar of the House. But there is nothing criminal in all this.

Mr. Wallace, in his speech, went on to say this, and I ask Hon. Members to take particular note of this assumption of the lawyer to give evidence on the matter: 'These articles and letters clearly indicate that the mass meeting which was to take place was to enforce the receiving of the deputation.' How did he know that? There is not a word in the article or in the letter about it. He went on to say: 'It is well known, from what has happened on former occasions, what is likely to happen when large numbers of unemployed and other people as well get together on instructions to present petitions to Parliament.' Really, we must look at this matter very closely, because if this is going to hold, then when the Labour people hold their demonstrations in February and want to send deputations to the House to interview members, the same treatment may be meted out to us. At any rate, we ought to have the same treatment if this policy is right. You have no right to deal with us differently. Therefore, I hope we shall face the situation. There are many precedents for sending men and women to the number of five to this House to see Hon. Members to put before them any statements they want to make.

The government bases their action on what happened in November; once bitten twice shy, these people called a demonstration and attempted to get into the House. But see what happened on this occasion – and what right have you to assume that it would not have happened with Tom Mann. He was one of the first to help to organize a May Day demonstration in this House when we split ourselves into groups of five and interviewed individual members. We got one of the best interviews on unemployment with the late Lord Salisbury and Mr. Balfour and Mr. Gladstone, arid one of the Liberal peers. That is the policy which Tom Mann might have followed if he had been given the opportunity, but as it was, he was in prison.

Mr. Saklatvala came to the House, brought his friends with him, and tried to see the Minister of Labour. He could not ask to see the Prime Minister, because he knew that he was not here. What right had he for his assumption? Where is the evidence upon which he based his assumption, except what had happened before? There is no evidence in the letter or in the article that this demonstration might not have been carried out in an entirely different manner. I defy the government to produce any evidence of the kind.

We have the evidence of what happened after the action of the government. Mr. Saklatvala came here in a perfectly orderly manner and attempted to get an interview. Detective Passmore gave evidence as to what happened at the last demonstration, but there is no evidence that Mr. Mann was there and no evidence was given that his friend was there. They are mere statements, no evidence at all.

Tom Mann made his speech, and this is what he said – there is not a scrap of evidence to controvert it. He did not participate in violence but merely took part in meetings, which were admittedly within the right of citizens. He held that these proceedings were entirely unwarranted. He looked upon them as part of the general procedure of the authorities against the workers' committee. His aim and object had been to get legitimate grievances remedied in a fair, straightforward, honest, and becoming fashion.

Llewellyn addressed the magistrate in the same way. He said that no violence had ever been advocated by him, and what violence had taken place was against innocent demonstrators. That is all the evidence.

Here is what the magistrate said, and I commend it to the notice of the Solicitor-General and the Home Secretary. Sir Chartres Biron, in making his decision, said there had been a misapprehension as to the nature of these proceedings. No criminal charge had been made and there was no question of imprisonment. The proceedings were merely putting in force the law which had been the law of the land from time immemorial and which had been held by judges on very recent occasions to be for the protection of public order. It was merely a preventive measure. In any condition he imposed on the defendants, there would be nothing which would in any way interfere with their legitimate activities. The only undertaking he called upon them to give would be merely in the interests of stopping disorder, of which both men said they entirely disapproved. As no one had proved anything to the contrary against them, why should the magistrate want them to enter into recognizances? There was not a scrap of evidence against them, and he accepts their word.

It was clear that there was a mass meeting announced and arranged for Monday, which was to present a petition to the House of Parliament. In his (the judge's) view there would be a mass mob within the vicinity of the House of Commons. How does he know? There is no evidence about it except what has happened on some other occasion. But, he charges the two men in some way with being responsible for this without a scrap of evidence that they were responsible. I come back to that again and again, because that is the gravamen of our charge against the government on this matter.

Then, he went on: 'There is nothing to prevent anyone presenting a petition to the House of Commons, but it is most undesirable that such a petition should be presented by an organized mass of people marching on the House of Commons.' Certainly, but there is no evidence to show that Tom Mann and Llewellyn had any such intention, and my case is that unless you can prove that intention, you had no right to arrest.

Then, he went on: 'It is common knowledge that this mass of people were meeting on Monday to make this mass demonstration under exactly the same conditions as a meeting in October, when there was great disorder.' I may be a very ignorant person, but until Tom Mann was arrested, I had no knowledge whatever that this demonstration was to be held, and I believe that the arrest of Tom Mann gave all the publicity that the Communist Party desired; it gave the meeting just the advertisement that it wanted. Here is the most astounding statement of the magistrate: he did not say that the present defendants were responsible for that. The magistrate admits that they were not responsible. Why should he have called upon them to enter into recognizances? But it showed what such meetings were likely to produce and against which had sworn to preserve the peace. But they have not produced a scintilla of evidence that these men were responsible in any way, and it is the magistrate who said it.

What I want to ask is, is it the law of the land? And does the Home Secretary consider that he is really going to maintain respect for the law, if a man can be put away in this way? It is all very well for the Right Hon. Gentleman to say, 'No honorable man would refuse to enter into recognizances.' The Right Hon. Gentleman knows very well that if any one of us was charged under these conditions, we never would give the undertaking.

We have become very mealy mouthed in these days in the press. In the old days, *Reynold's Newspaper* used to publish much more seditious matter than this and never be attacked. The *National Reformer*, which was a Republican paper, used to attack the Crown and the princes and the princesses when they were getting married, used to attack the allowances, and so on. *The Impeachment of the House of Brunswick* was published, also the *Secret History of the Court of England*, and last, *The Carson Campaign*.

It is all very well for Hon. and Right Hon. Gentleman to laugh about it now, but in those days it was a serious matter, and when I say that this is class persecution, I am stating only what the facts prove.

116

I was a member of this House during most of this period, and everyone knows that at that time, the government did not dare to interfere with a test mobilization of the Ulster volunteers who landed a huge consignment of 40,000 German Mauser rifles at Larne. I do not know what the position of the present Home Secretary was in those days. If he was in the Tory Party, he was up to his neck in it, and he is no sort of judge in this business at all. Under the able leadership of the late Lord Londonderry, the Ulstermen, with the assistance of Lord Carson, organized an army of 100,000 men. They set up a provisional government. They told the people in Ulster that the German Kaiser would come and help them if ever they were handed over, and so on. They organized a mutiny in the British Army which caused one war secretary to resign and the Prime Minister to take his place. All this was done, and I believe it was the beginning of the sort of action that you are complaining about today. It proves that in this country there is one law for the rich and another for the poor. It shows that Right Hon. Gentlemen, like the Home Secretary and those who acted together in the years 1910 to 1914 to stop the Home Rule Bill passing, did not mind what they did, and no government dared interfere.

Here is what one of the leaders said: 'At the present moment, the weapons are under the control of the leaders. The moment a raid for arms is made, there will be an order for a general assembly.' Here is what Lord Carson said, and he was never prosecuted: 'I do not hesitate to tell you that you ought to set yourselves against the constituted authority in the land.' No communist has stated anything worse than that.

We will set up a government. I am told it will be illegal. Of course it will. Drilling is illegal. Volunteers are illegal. The government knows they are illegal. The government dare not interfere with them. Of course they dare not, because they were rich and well-to-do and powerful people. Do not be afraid of illegalities. Illegalities are not crimes when they are taken to assert what is the elementary right of every citizen, the protection of his freedom. It is the doctrine of the communists today – and it is my doctrine – that the first elementary right of a man is that he shall be able to earn his daily bread and live in decency and comfort. These other people were only fighting for political rights, but they were not interfered with. It is only a crime to commit illegalities when you commit them for bread. But that fight is over. The people who fought that fight under Lord Londonderry and Lord Carson won. They won because they took advantage of the fact that this nation was at war, and they brought about by their action the terrible conditions that prevailed in Ireland during the last years of the War and immediately afterwards.

If this is going to remain the law of the land, then the people of the world will know that this great and powerful nation has one law with which to deal with poor people struggling for the right to earn their daily bread and another law for the well-to-do. I do not agree that the Communist Party represents more than a small fraction of the people, but they and those who gather around them are calling attention to the fact that, in this the richest country in the world, there are about 3,000,000 people, sometimes more, sometimes less, living on the verge of destitution.

The government is doing in this matter what all cowardly governments do. They are resorting to suppression. They are mixing suppression with a sort of pseudo-charity. The Prime Minister's broadcast defined the government's policy as a policy which said: 'We are going to rely on private charity and private benefactions.' That speech was made over the wireless, and it has been impossible to reply to it, because the British Broadcasting Corporation arrogates to itself the right to decide who shall speak over the wireless, when they shall speak, and what they shall say on political questions of the day. If the Prime Minister and the government had chosen, they could have used the goodwill in the country, the real downright generous feeling that exists among multitudes of men and women, to deal with the momentary difficulties which are being suffered today by so many people. If the Prime Minister had been true to any of the teachings which he himself has taught in this country, if he had been true to the faith he held for many years, he could also have harnessed that goodwill to fundamental changes in the conditions that produce poverty and distress.

The organized workers have a right to say to the government that they will have nothing to do with this attempt to put on to the shoulders of decent, generous-hearted people a responsibility which belongs to the government. In dealing with these people as the government are dealing with them, the government are accentuating class hatred and class bitterness by proving once more that you treat the weaker people, the communists, the Labour people – even when they break the law ever so little – in a fashion altogether different from that in which you deal with the rich and well-to-do. The history of the last 20 years proves it, and the example of the Right. Hon. Gentleman himself proves it. It is no use saying: 'That was a good cause and this is a bad cause.' Illegality is illegality whether it is committed by a Lord of Appeal, Lord Carson, and the Home Secretary, or whether it is committed by Tom Mann and Llewellyn.

2.11 p.m.

Buchanan: I think the Right Hon. Gentleman has covered almost every aspect of this question, but there are one or two matters to which I should like to direct the attention of the House. In connection with the case against Mrs. Duncan, I wish to mention what occurred in a case heard at Birmingham a few weeks ago. I, of course, am not going to discuss here the details of that case in Birmingham, but it was a trial for murder, the most serious indictment that could be laid against any citizen. I say this to the credit of the legal profession that, in that case, a learned counsel for whom we have very high regard and who formerly sat with the Liberal Party in this House – Mr. Birkett – went down to defend. I suggest that the two gentlemen in charge of this debate ought to have regard to what happened in that case at Birmingham.

Incidentally, I would say to legal gentlemen that they ought to have a very deep regard for the rights of the people in carrying out the law. I think if a man has dislikes, and we have all our likes and dislikes, he ought to take all the greater care in seeing that justice is carried out in the cases of those for whom he may have any dislike. I remember a home secretary who is a Jew saying to me that he was very diffident about acting in a case of a member of his own race, but in the cases of other people, he went to the utmost extremes to give them the benefit of the doubt, and I think that that was good. In this Birmingham

119

case to which I have referred, certain notes were given in evidence, and the judge, in summing up, pointed out that the notes had not been taken at the time of the alleged statement, but had been written afterwards. Mr. Birkett, for the defense, was able to convince the judge and a jury of his fellow countrymen of the righteousness of his case on this point, and the judge made some very pointed remarks on the nature of the evidence and gave a certain instruction to the jury.

I do not wish to labor the point, but I would point out its application to the case against Mrs. Duncan. In the case at Birmingham, it was only a matter of a short conversation and a comparatively few words. But when a person is charged with making certain statements in a speech, lasting perhaps an hour, the point is even stronger. How is evidence to be given of that, except by means of notes of the whole speech? One may get two or three words exactly as they are spoken in a speech, but the context may entirely change the meaning of those words. How often in this House do we hear a member following another member in debate and unintentionally taking quite a wrong meaning from some words of the previous speech. But here you have an instance of the liberty of the subject being jeopardized because of evidence of that kind being laid against a defendant. I say that to imprison anyone. And to ask for security on evidence of that kind is entirely wrong.

I am not a lawyer, but I think I know just a little about it. Hitherto, in the courts which I have attended – and I have watched some of the so-called worst criminals being tried – I have constantly watched the judge being fair to the defense. In Scotland, we lay it down that it is the procurator's duty not to prosecute, but to see that the facts are brought out. Particularly is that impressed upon him in the case of people who are poor. It is constantly emphasized that everything in favor of the defendant shall be stated. Here, not one single thing was brought out in the case of Mrs. Duncan; nothing about her past life. As the Hon. Member for Bridgeton (Mr. Maxton) knows, she is Scot and has a good record of public service. Nothing of that was brought out. All that is allowed in a court of law is evidence. I have been in a court when the recorder at the Old Bailey has said: 'We are not here to deal with what you think; we are here to deal with evidence. You can say what you like, but you must say it on oath.' The notes of the case are handed up to the judge. Judges may be great, but they have no right to take into consideration a single thing unless it is sworn on oath.

I do not share the contempt about solicitors and counsel that is often popularly voiced. I am indebted to the man from Birmingham I spoke about for defending a constituent of mine – possibly the kindest thing a man has ever done without fee, without press, without anything.

I have seen even poor solicitors working night and day for people from whom they have no hope of getting any reward. I appeal to them, for the sake of their profession, to see that people are properly tried and given justice. How can you get it when the evidence is not real evidence? What right has the learned magistrate to read from notes not sworn on oath? What right have you to cross-examine on that? The trial of that woman would never have been tolerated in any court if the charge had only been ordinary theft, or even a grave charge of murder. The whole thing was done in an atmosphere of sentence before trial.

There is another point. It is no defense to plead ignorance of the law in this country. On the other hand, it is constantly being taken as good law that the law has a reasonable chance of being assimilated by the citizens. How could anybody say that a statute of King Edward III – I forget the date quoted – could, with any shadow of reason, be known by any poor person. It had hardly ever been invoked within recent times. While judges may have given decisions on certain matters, that statute had not been invoked, and no poor man had a reasonable chance of assimilating the law, or of understanding even that there was such a law, and yet the prosecution was taken under it.

I do not want to bear out the characters given by the previous speaker, other than to say I know Llewellyn and I know Tom Mann. He was general secretary of the Amalgamated Engineers' Union. I am chairman of the Pattern Makers'; and he and I were associated for some years and worked together. I do not know much about his speaking. I never heard him speak on a public platform. But he was a most moderate man when I met him and was looked upon as a much more moderate man than I was in the councils of the engineering trade. He was looked upon as capable and clean in conduct.

Llewellyn, I have met many times. He is an ordinary, decent Welsh chap, with no side about him; an ordinary man of the sort that might be taken from the Welsh coalfields any day in the year. I say the whole attitude is wrong about this so-called disorder outside the House recently. I was present. The Hon. Member for Bridgton would have gone with me, but for the fact that as his appearance is so well known, the crowd would have known him. I went down to the crowd just to see what was happening. I went through Whitehall right from Trafalgar Square. I met the Hon. Member for Shettleston (Mr. McGovern), and he and I took diverse ways and met again. We went down to Victoria and along the embankment. I have seen many Orange demonstrations in Glasgow 60 times worse than anything connected with that demonstration, particularly at night, when two or three spirits get to work. That is nothing against the organizers, who are clean and decent men. I have seen Orange demonstrations in Glasgow where there have been dozens of ambulances out. I have seen them at Anderson Cross. I went through the whole thing when the demonstration was outside here, and the only untoward incident I saw – and I think a Conservative member would bear me out in this – was a special constable acting in a manner most – well, I cannot properly describe it. I say this to the credit of the police, that they took the matter in hand and acted with discretion. That demonstration was nothing to be annoyed about.

I think you have lost your nerve. You are in a funk. There is nobody who has any shred of imagination but knows that the Prime Minister has left us because he does not want to come. In seven weeks, he may feel better. Why should we not say it? If a man who was unemployed made the journey to Lossiemouth overnight, hundreds of miles, they would not, under the National Health Insurance scheme, accept that as a reason for giving benefit, and it is no use our treating well-to-do men differently from the way in which we treat poor people. The whole thing is wrong. I know the Home Secretary better than does the leader of the opposition. He and I are kindred members, and have been associated for many years in public life, and I know there is not much use making an appeal to him.

But I do appeal to the legal people, not because they are members of the government, but for the sake of their profession. I earnestly appeal to them to see that the liberties of these men and women are safeguarded at this time.

After all, you would not have done it to the leaders of the Labour movement, because if you had, you know you would at once have made these men the greatest men in the movement. It is done because these people are in a small minority, or it is thought they are. It is thought they are unpopular, and you are taking action against them that is fundamentally wrong. The thing that arouses me is this, that it is not done fairly and with decency and credit. None of those people got the trial that they should have got, and I hope the Home Secretary will say that he thinks this prosecution was mistakenly undertaken, and that the trial of Mrs. Duncan was not conducted in a way that did credit to law and justice in this country. I hope that, as Home Secretary, he will take the necessary action to overturn those decisions and that he will act a manly part, not only for his own sake and for the sake of his office, but above all, for the sake of giving justice a decent name in this country.

2.28 p.m.

Sir John Gilmour – Tory MP and Minister: The last thing I should desire to do would be to introduce any heat into this discussion. But the Hon. Member for Gorbals (Mr. Buchanan), who has just addressed the House, has, as he frankly said, been known to me, and we have known each other and represented constituencies in Glasgow alongside each other for a number of years. He has said a great many things today about the proper conduct of trials, and anybody might be in agreement with perhaps a great deal of what fell from him. But I must join issue at once with him when he asks me to say that the trial which was conducted in dealing with Mrs. Duncan was improperly done, or that there was distinct unfairness on the part of Mr. Wallace. I would say, frankly, that this is not the place in which trials before courts should be reviewed. It is most unsuitable, and I suppose that, at any rate, it will be recognized that men like Mr. Wallace, who have these grave responsibilities, have every right to be protected against assertions to which they cannot reply.

James Maxton – Socialist and seen as far-left and colorful; Labour MP, Glasgow: Are you supposed to defend them?

Gilmour: I was given notice by the Right Hon. Gentleman opposite, at a late hour last night, of this particular case. I immediately, of course, made inquiries and obtained, within the time at my disposal, such information as I could about the case. Whether it be this case or the cases of Tom Mann and Llewellyn, I want to bring the House back to the position in which any officer in any executive position stands who has to deal with these problems at the present time. I, for the time being, occupy this post, and I want to assure the House of Commons, and any who may be critics of what I may do, that the one thing above all which I desire to avoid is to allow circumstances to develop into a position in which I shall require to use the forces at my disposal and not only involve my executive and my officers in grave risks, but bring about a conflict and a clash of forces in the streets of this metropolis which can only end in bringing disaster to many people, not only those who are guilty of incitement, but those who in many cases are the dupes of those people.

It is no use saying to me that the action which has been taken is based upon some ancient and antiquated law. It is based upon the practice of many generations, it is true, and it is linked, no doubt, with ancient laws. But it is connected and linked also with the practice of the law coming right up to modern times.

Maxton: How can you say that?

Gilmour: It is clear that in certain cases which have taken place in this country in recent times, to which the Right Hon. Gentleman opposite referred, those cases were restated by the law at that time. This House knows well the possibilities of those outside coming to this House and presenting petitions, and it was only on the occasion of the last disturbance that the Hon. Member representing the Shettleston Division of Glasgow (Mr. McGovern) got into touch with those very people upon this particular subject. He was prepared to place his services at their disposal in order that they might, through the proper channels, make their representations. We all know that the statement which that Hon. Member made to this House was a thankless and, if I may say so, a proper appreciation of the situation, which was greatly to his credit. The fact remains…

Maxton: The people wanted to do it themselves.

Gilmour: But they wanted to do it in a manner which is well known as contrary to the rules, either of this House or of decent, orderly methods.

Maxton: No, nothing of the sort. These men took the view that, if this petition was to be presented here, they were going to do it through their own organization and not through any assistance from us or Hon. Gentlemen above the gangway. It was a perfectly legitimate view.

Gilmour: Let me quote the words of the Hon. Member for Shettleston: 'Having met Mr. Wal Hannington and Mr. Harry McShane on Friday, and made that offer to them, on behalf of the unemployed hunger marchers I have been informed this morning by Mr. McShane that their council discussed the offer yesterday, and decided to reject this necessary medium and to rely on their massed strength to force Parliament to allow their deputation to appear at the Bar.' (Official Report, 31st October, 1932; col. 1445, vol. 269)

Maxton: You rely on your massed strength.

Gilmour: I want the House to realize the position of responsibility in which I am placed by such words. This is not my interpretation, but the interpretation of the Hon. Member for Shettleston, which was made to this House and is on record. That mass force and that large concourse of people led, as we know on the previous occasion, to grave disorders in the streets of London.

Maxton: Where?

Gilmour: It led to disorders in Hyde Park; it dislocated the whole of the traffic throughout London; it led to the necessary calling out of large numbers of police and special constables; and it involved the necessity of envisaging, on the part of those responsible for law and order, that if the forces that were called upon were unable to cope with the large masses of people, it would be essential to call out the military. The House will believe me when I say that neither this government nor I, personally, have the slightest desire to employ repressive measures either against freedom of speech or the proper passage of regular and orderly processions. But, when I am told that these processions are being deliberately organized for the purpose of avoiding the proper presentation of their petitions, and that they intend to come in such large forces as to intimidate this House, I am bound to take action.

Some reference has been made to some of my colleagues and myself as having got cold feet. My responsibility is to see that law and order is kept, whatever class is concerned; and I want to say that I make no differentiation between the orderly conduct of people, to whatever class they may belong. And those who break the law and disobey the orders of the House are bound to be dealt with.

Lansbury: Except Ulstermen.

Gilmour: Let me deal with what is before the House. The fact remains that this body, the National Unemployed Workers' Movement, did organize a mass procession. The House is aware of the result. We saw the disorders; we saw the train of trouble and difficulty which arose from them; and we saw the deluded people who were carried in the train of that disturbance. If I am convinced of one thing more than another, it is that the methods of disorderly concourse which were arranged by the organizers and members of that body are out of tune with and against the interests of the decent working man. What the unemployed want is not mass demonstration but work, and it is not by disorderly or intimidatory methods that they are going to get that out of this government or, indeed, any other government. Those who take part in such proceedings defeat their object.

With regard to the case of Tom Mann and Llewellyn, all I can say is that they were asked, as many other people may be asked, either now or in the future, to give an undertaking that they will not conduct themselves or incite others to conduct themselves in a manner other than orderly and properly. Is it to be said that it is not proper to ask these men to give this undertaking? If that be so, the only alternative which the executive has is to recognize, well knowing that these disorders are bound to come, that they must leave the methods of the organizers to develop and to bring out the police force again and again in order to carry out the orders of this House. Within the precincts of the Houses of Parliament, the police are directed under my care to see that no disturbance occurs. If this

House is going to abrogate its rights to issue those instructions, good and well, but as long as these instructions are issued to me, it is my duty to see that they are carried out; and the only way in which I can carry them out is by inviting those who have published that they are going to bring people in a demonstration in large masses within the precincts...

Lansbury: May I ask the Right Hon. Gentleman kindly to tell the House what evidence he has connecting Tom Mann with the *Daily Worker*, what evidence there is that he had anything to do with writing or publishing that article, and what there is wrong in the letter that he wrote to the Prime Minister? Does the Right Hon. Gentleman maintain that he must take people up without giving evidence of intent on their part or of any action that they have taken which leads him to think that they ought to be put under recognizances?

Gilmour: When the last disturbance occurred, the step which has now been taken was not taken. These disturbances led to very grave disorder, and they placed a great strain upon the police and upon law and order. When it was apparent, from information of which I was made aware, that there would be another demonstration, which was announced in the press – which was, in fact, a repetition of the attempt to bring this petition, signed by a million people, to the precincts of this House, not through the ordinary methods of which the House is well aware, but by exactly the same methods as on the previous occasion – it was obvious that the attempt was being organized and directed by the association of which Toni Mann and Llewellyn were members...

Lansbury: You have not a scrap of evidence of that.

Gilmour: Let me put this to the House. This particular case was taken through the proper channels. The defendants were brought to the court, and as far as I know, they never denied that there was justification for their being brought into court. What they refused to do there was to give a plain and perfectly simple undertaking that they would not carry out what the law said they ought not to do.

McEntee, Labour MP, Walthamstow: They were not charged with that.

127

Gilmour: Of course, they were not accused of that, but it was made clear that all they were asked was that they would behave themselves as orderly citizens of this country.

Lansbury: The point is, the Right Hon. Gentleman has built up his case against these two men on what happened previously. The magistrate himself said that he did not hold these two men responsible for what happened in November.

Gilmour: Whether that was so or not, the whole position is this: that if we had a repetition of what happened before, it was going to lead to very grave disorders. In an endeavor to prevent it, these men are asked to give undertakings that they will not incite or take part in any such disorderly proceedings. Is it too much to ask? [Hon. Members: 'Yes!'] That is the object with which this action was taken – to prevent a repetition of these disturbances, which I think are contrary to the desire and wish not only of the unemployed, but of every decent citizen in the country.

All I have got to say is this, that I believe that we were within our rights, that what we did was calculated to cause less disturbance – it was done for that reason and that reason alone – and that these men could have given the undertaking, which was no outrageous undertaking and one which they could have given without any dereliction of their position, without giving away any right of proper free speech or attendance at political meetings. They refused to do it, and they have suffered the consequences. In both cases, I have no reason to think that justice has not been carried out, and I do not propose to release them.

Maxton: What about Mrs. Duncan?

LLOYD GEORGE: Prime Minister, I do not propose to continue the exhaustive discussion, which has been carried on during the last few hours.

Chapter Seven

Best Friends – Fred Copeman and the Invergordon Mutiny

In 1935, the first blockbuster movie, about HMS Bounty, was made. It told the story of crewmembers mutinying against their cruel Captain Bligh, and the heroic way in which he rowed his tiny boat thousands of miles to hunt down his former mutinous crew. The film started Charles Laughton and Clark Gable, two of the biggest Hollywood movie stars of the age. In 1962, *Mutiny on the Bounty* was again recreated for the big screen; also with the biggest movie stars of the age in the key roles: Marlon Brando, Trevor Howard, and Richard Harris. As recently as 1984, the film was remade as *The Bounty*, starring Mel Gibson and Anthony Hopkins.

Films about rebellion and mutiny are often very popular and can be extremely lucrative for the studios who make them; but they can also serve another purpose: to get it firmly into the public's mind that disobedience and rebellion are not acceptable and never successful, and that, if you do rebel, you will be punished and hunted down. Conversely, leaders who know better will always control the power, and consequently the media and state narrative. Up to the present (2018), I have yet to see any of the many remakes of Mutiny at Invergordon.

I have lost track of the big names that must have starred in this amazing true story; the Oscar awards that have been showered upon it; and the endless books and classroom debates about the two days, 15 and 16 September, 1931, when the British Navy mutinied and the government had to agree to its terms or fall from office. One of the leaders of the mutiny was Kath Duncan's best friend, Fred Copeman, who had been raised in a workhouse and had joined the navy as a way of escaping to a better life.

Fred Copeman probably first came across Kath Duncan whilst on leave, in 1928, and visiting a friend in Camberwell.

Kath, although still living in Hackney at this time, was gaining national prominence for her street rallies and protests; and her great beauty and wit not only would draw huge crowds everywhere she went, but were also the talk of people both above stairs and below.

Fred, after a lifetime in the workhouse, had chosen the Navy as his way out, and after gunnery school, joined the *Norfolk*, a brand-new cruiser in the Atlantic fleet. This was in 1931, when the financial crisis back in Britain was at its greatest. Talk of cuts was widespread, and the armed forces and the navy would have to take their fair share of them. The newspapers circulating onboard ships gave the actual reductions as: Admiral 7%, Lieutenant Commander 3.7%, Chief Petty Officer 11.8%, and able seamen, including Fred, a whopping 23% of what was already a very low rate that barely provided sustenance. Married men struggled the hardest, taking on other jobs to eke out a living, such as doing others' laundry or working as a barber, tailor, or other professions. When the ship docked in port, many would never disembark, only too aware that leaving the ship would mean seeing what little they had spent in the docks' bars and brothels. Whilst the Navy was expected to take £3 million in cuts, mainly through staff wage reductions, the crew could see for themselves that large savings could be made by reducing the lengths of cruises the ships took, thus saving oil and coal costs. Suddenly, talk on ship was becoming less about sport, women, and song, and more about politics. Fred was not the only crewmember who had heard about the rise of the Communist and Labour Parties on the mainland and its activists and speakers, like Kath Duncan, who were so able to articulate their thoughts and feelings.

Fred and Kitty Copeman and family

Whilst 15 and 16 September are the dates recognized for the mutiny, the real trouble started on Saturday, 12 September, 1931, during a naval competitive event called the Fleet Cup Final, between Fred's ship, the *Nelson*, and the *Dorchester*. The rest of the fleet was in dock and their crews were on shore, watching the event, having drinks, and chatting. As the night drew in, a fight broke out between some drunken ship hands and some officers; this in itself was rare, but seemed to pass off.

The main canteen on the dock was packed with crews at a time when, normally, they would be heading back to their ships. Able Seaman Bond, of Fred's ship, the *Nelson*, got up on a table and addressed the packed room, "What the hell are you going to do about it? These cuts – are we going to sit down and take them?"

At first, through fear, and probably driven by the courage one-too-many beers can give all men, the debate was more about people stating their grievances. As more and more spoke, a proposal was put forward that all the seaman should stay on shore and sleep in the canteen overnight. However, as it was winter and cold, the idea was dropped, as was a proposal to march to Glasgow. With no agreement, the crews returned to their ships, angry but in need of space to sleep off what many had thought was far too much beer.

On Sunday, the Port Watch arrived on shore and the word about the previous day's events had rapidly spread through the fleet, and so another meeting naturally ensued, with less beer to blur the mind. At this meeting, the men decided that they should take soundings from all the crews as to what action, if any, they should and could take, and the meeting came to an end.

On Monday, Fred was due for his shore leave from the *Nelson*, and within just an hour of the latest meeting having started, an Officer of the Guard came into the meeting and read the Riot Act. This was ill-timed and turned disgruntled sailors into men with a very serious decision to make.

The canteen was so packed that the decision was made to move the meeting to Black Park, a football ground close by that had a raised stage area and enough room for everyone to see, hear, and take part in the debate. Wincott was a fellow seaman from the *Norfolk* and was on the stage when he noticed Fred, a tall, imposing figure, standing at the front of the stage. "Why don't you tell them what you think, Fred?"

Before Fred knew what was happening, he found himself pushed up a ladder and onto the stage. Fred had some idea of politics from his new, but brief, friendship with Kath Duncan. She, at 5-feet-2-inches, was a giant on the stage; yet he, at 6 feet and with a boxer's build, felt small. Through Kath's speeches, he understood the issues and had seen how best to address a crowd that felt badly robbed of justice, as his Navy chums did now. Looking out into the huge crowd, Fred had flashes of what he felt he needed to say and the spirit of Kath to say what needed to be said.

Turning to the crowd, Fred started his first ever public speech and the die was cast. "If you want to hear what I've got to say, then for Christ's sake pipe down. So long as we are agreed that the cuts in their present form are unjust, there remains the problem of what to do about it. It seems to me that it's time we expressed our opinions in a more organized way, and I propose that you return to your ships and see that the Port Watch act with us. It will be foolish for us to do anything here without the other half of the men knowing what it is all about. Sleeping in the canteen is daft, and to try to march down to Glasgow is even madder. We are sailors, not soldiers, and our strength is in the fleet itself. Whatever we do, everybody must be in it. There must be no question of splitting one section from another. The mariners must enter this fight with us at the beginning." Fred had made his first public speech, and it would lead to him becoming one of the most important rebels of his age. His speech had led a disorganized rabble to agree as comrades that they would strike.

It's no easy task trying to call a strike across an entire fleet when, in 1931, you do not have the joy and accessibility of social media to mobilize your forces.

The plan was agreed that everyone should ignore the first morning's ship's call, and that all crewmembers should gather on deck, with all ships acting as one. Fred and Wincott moved amongst their crew on the *Nelson*, urging them to go up on the recreation deck, where the plan of action would be laid before them. This space was the largest clear space and common ground on the ship, and Wincott and Fred started telling everyone what had been agreed and pleading for solidarity. No one would be victimized if they chose not to take part, and it was a huge relief when Fred asked the mariners whether they were with him, yes or no, and they spoke up with one voice: 'Yes.'

A strike committee was immediately set up, and Fred, who through his sporting prowess was known by every crewmember on every ship, became acutely aware that there was no turning back. Fred was filled with terror at what they were about to do, whilst being thrilled at how successful their action was looking.

There was no turning back. The strike committee would need to work immediately to organize and oversee the day-to-day operations of the fleet. Who was to cook the food? Who was to man the picket boats? What jobs could be done, and by whom?

It was agreed that every section would take a share of the workload but would not follow a full normal shift. The officers would be free to move about the ship as usual, although one striker yelled out, "Who's going to peel their spuds?"

And the crowd replied, "They'll peel their ruddy own, or the snotties will do it for them."

As morning arrived on the *Norfolk*, the wireless operators had communicated between all the ships in the fleet that each ship would muster on the fo'c'sle. Then, starting with the ships right out at the harbor mouth, cheers would be heard from each ship that was with Fred and his mutineers.

As the ships stretched in double lines out to sea, with smaller ships inshore, the scariest moment in Fred's life had arrived. The next five minutes could decide if he would be arrested or shot and if his rebellion, the greatest act of independence ever organized in the Navy, would be a success or failure.

Fear gripped the strike leaders as tension mounted: Would any ship's crew cheer? Would any crew really mutiny without a beer to give them courage? The agreed time passed, and the air was silent. Then, quite suddenly, a roar in the distance was heard. Instead of waiting for each ship to cheer on cue, the entire fleet cheered as one. For 5 or 10 minutes, 15,000 members of the King's Navy were cheering and celebrating mutiny. The entire fleet was in solidarity.

Word quickly arrived that the admiral of the fleet had given instructions that the *Valiant* and *Rodney* proceed to sea for independent maneuvers, which all present clearly saw as an attempt to break the strike. As tension grew, news came in that as officers were raising the starboard anchor, the ship's company were dropping the port one. With both anchors down, the Commander-in-Chief issued orders cancelling the planned maneuvers. The attempt to break the strike had failed.

The wireless operators sent out their demands to the admiralty in London.

'We, the loyal subjects of His Majesty, the King, do hereby present to the Lords Commissioners of the Admiralty our earnest representations to them to revise the drastic cuts in pay that have been inflicted upon the lowest paid men of the lower deck. It is evident to all concerned that these cuts are the forerunner of tragedy, poverty, and immorality amongst the families of the men of the lower deck. The men are quite willing to accept cuts, which they, the men, think within reason, and unless this is done, we must remain as one unit, refusing to serve under the rates of pay.'

Fred, always taking the side of caution and mindful that what they were doing could see all of the strike leadership lined up and shot, also ensured that the press was informed. These were early days, and Fred knew he needed the public to be aware. He wanted their concerns and the reason for the strike to reach the public before the government could have time to block the press and stop their action from being made public.

Kath was one of the first to get the news that her new best friend, Fred, had just caused a revolution of his own, without her, and was leading a 15,000-strong contingent of sailors who were demanding fair pay and fair working conditions. Kath's thoughts were probably a mixture of real excitement and pride but also terror at the thought of what could become of Fred and the leadership if the public was not bought on side.

The government in London held two emergency cabinet meetings and agreed to the strikers' terms and not to carry out any victimization of its leadership. Fred's fellow rebel leader, Wincott, was loath to trust the promise that none of them would face trial. He was well-read and knew only too well the fate of other British mutineers such as those on the *Nore*, who had all ended up hanged.

The condition of the agreement was that the ships would return to Plymouth and the sailors would be given leave. As Fred's ship, the *Norfolk*, sailed into port, the *Plymouth Hoe* was packed with people. The red banners of the Communist Party waved in the crowd, which would include a coachload of comrades from Deptford that Kath had organized as a welcome home.

After the arrival in Plymouth, the admiralty was quick to move and dispersed the 15,000-strong crew across the rest of the Navy. The first people transferred were Fred Copeman, A.B Wincott, and Ginger Ladd from the *Norfolk*. No one was hanged or shot, and no one faced trial.

Three weeks later, Fred Copeman, who had requested a discharge from the Navy three years earlier but had been refused, found himself being called to the guardroom, where an officer of the guard informed him that his discharge had been granted. The actions of the admiralty were universally regarded as petty, and collections were made in the pubs in Davenport and Plymouth for the small group of men who, without the Navy, had no homes; even the prostitutes gave generously to the collections. The men had their lives and their liberty, and they had not been kicked out in disgrace. They were, to a man, real men of honor.

The Communist Party had been made aware of the mutiny in error. The scale of the mutiny across the entire fleet had led the government and the establishment media to think that it was not possible for able seamen on their own to organize such an event on such a scale so quickly. As with the fall of Russia, it was not the first Russian revolution of March 1917 they feared, but Lenin's Revolution in the October of 1917.

Lenin's popularity in the West had seen the rise of the British Communist Party in 1920 and its high-profile campaigns, such as the Hunger Strike marches and the 1926 General Strike, which showed that they were more than capable of bringing down the government. The general election of 1931 had also seen the first Communist MP elected to parliament, another friend of Kath Duncan, William (Bill) Gallagher. His success was partly due to Kath, who had left fighting her own seat in Greenwich to return to Kirkcaldy in order to mobilize support for him among her people. The admiralty had a different perspective. They had not forgotten that the fall of Germany in World War I had not been due to its being defeated in battle, but the fact that the German Navy had mutinied. History, in their mind's eye, was being repeated and had to be stopped.

The national newspapers were quick to report the aftermath of the Invergordon Mutiny with a new fleet order which the admiralty reckoned to be watertight. A foolproof gag on any expression of lower-deck opinion or needs was to be posted but would take until 1935 to be enshrined in law.

Although the government had to give way on the question of cuts during the 1931 mutiny, the admiralty, in a panic, took steps to ensure that, as soon as the fleet was safely split up, in future, the lower decks would have the minimum of opportunity for getting together to air their grievances. Their lordships announced that the then-existing system of welfare conferences would be abolished and directed that a review of service conditions should replace them. Their lordships further stated that, in order to be entirely satisfactory, such a review must be expeditious. 'Expeditious' was putting it mildly, reported the press, which was remarkable; the entire establishment media had sided with the 15,000 lower deck hands who had brought the Navy to its knees in a mutiny that almost brought down the government.

Dated July and with the imposing classification (* 1672.N.267 /354/7/ 1935), the new order challenged an existing system of ships' welfare conferences, under Article 12 of the King's Regulations and Admiralty Instructions, which permitted, at stated intervals, meetings to discuss matters affecting the lower deck. Written statements were also allowed to be prepared. The new fleet orders declared that a review of service conditions made meetings and the preparation of statements unnecessary, and that the regulation would be cancelled.

Ironically, the truth of the matter was that, since Invergordon, for all practical purposes, the regulation had been almost non-existent.

An outstanding point of the new order was that it would be forbidden to organize meetings to bring forward questions on conditions. Instead, on a date selected by the senior officer of each fleet, divisional officers would explain to their men the 'opportunity' which was afforded to them to put forward representations. Divisional requests would be formulated under the presidency of the divisional officer, by representatives of each division, who would be selected by the divisional officers themselves. The representations would then go through a whole series of further siftings, but the people on the committees doing the sifting would, in every case, be the same. These committees could call before them officers and ratings whose views they might wish to hear. However, if you were a lower deck sailor and had views, and you wanted the admiralty to hear them, you would have to be sure, after being duly careful to avoid discussions with your fellow sailors, that your views did not come under certain headings. The fleet order declared that some areas were to be regarded as outside the scope of the review – such as policy and discipline, or the general arrangements of duties in the navy.

Both the response to the mutiny itself and the new fleet orders clearly revealed the attitude of the admiralty and of the government to those who wanted to challenge injustice; and they were reported with outrage in the press.

The Communist Party did all that they could to capitalize on the mutiny, although Kath was far from happy that her friendship with Fred was being used in such a way. There were other strike leaders, so why Fred? After all, Fred was not a member of the Party and her own husband had been treated very badly by the organization – he had been expelled for having been a member of the Conservative Party for four weeks when he was a teenager. Now, the Communist Party were on her doorstep, seeking to claim the entire fleet mutiny as an event created by communist activists, which Kath and everyone else at the top of the Communist Party knew to be untrue. Later, Fred would write about his anger at the way this people's mutiny, in his mind, was hijacked by the Party. The Invergordon Mutiny came into being from the spontaneous reactions of the men of the fleet against injustice, and, as Fred would later write, it had nothing to do with any ideology or party politics.

For Fred, this was a turning point. He had discovered he had leadership potential, and that he could understand the politics of it all. He moved into 68 Ommaney Road, with Kath and Sandy and Mama. The Communist Party were quick to observe this. Fred and Kath were the new golden team of the Communist Party, and nothing would be the same again.

Just weeks later, Kath's friend, Winston Churchill, while on an American lecture tour and probably having just raised a whisky to 'That Kath,' rather relieved that the Invergordon mutiny had not taken place while he was in office, was struck by a car and almost killed on Fifth Avenue in New York.

Chapter Eight
Fighting Fascists and Falling out with Communists

Kath had very much her own clear idea of whom she felt were the victims of social injustice and inequality. It was not, as seemed to be the main view of the Communist Party, just white, straight men whose needs were not being addressed. For Kath, the working class and the poor also included women, children, gays, and people of all colors and of all faiths and none. She strongly believed that, and that if a people's revolution could be truly secured, it would only come about by these groups uniting in solidarity.

Although she rose rapidly through the ranks and was, by the 1930s, the country's most famous communist, Kath always found the restrictions and ideology-driven leadership difficult and challenging. This was not helped when her husband, Sandy Duncan, was expelled from the Communist Party after it had been discovered that he had briefly been a member of the Young Conservatives in his youth. Even then, however, his activism and loyalty to the party could not be undermined. Sandy accepted his removal and worked hard to ensure that Kath would stay within the organization, always supporting her, come what may. No longer being a paid-up member of the Communist Party would not put an end to his activism, and he still, proudly, like Kath, held on to his National Union of Teachers membership card.

By the 1931 General Election, the country was in its worst crisis since the Great War. Despite having been told that winning the war would create a better world for everyone, only the rich, in Kath's eyes, were doing well, on the blood, sweat, and labor of the people she cared about. Therefore, being asked to stand for parliament in the Greenwich seat as the official Communist Party candidate – and the only woman one – was a badge of honor she would be proud to wear. The meeting to endorse Kath Duncan, who was also, by this stage, a member of the ruling executive of the Communist Party, was held at Borough Hall, on Royal Hill, Greenwich. The room was decked out with red flags, pictures of Lenin, and slogans in Russian and Chinese. The stage, like the rest of the hall, had been carefully decorated with the Deptford and Greenwich Communist Party flag, with its image of Lenin surrounded with a wreath of yellow corn. Hanging over the chairman's table was a red embroidered cloth with inscriptions in Russian and English; and in the center was an object representing the world dominated by the sickle and the hammer.

On each side of the stage hung banners with the slogans *Workers of the World Unite,* repeated in Russian and French; and others were emblazoned in large Chinese and Japanese characters on a blood-red background. Kath appeared on the platform carrying a bouquet of bright red asters, her favorite flower.

DEPTFORD DISPERSES FASCISTS

Meeting Mastered By Workers

THE Blackshirts invaded Deptford on Saturday night, but were soon forced to beat a strategic and undignified retreat.

They had previously been stopped from holding meetings at Deptford, but for a week they were loudly boasting that they would invade the Red stronghold and mop up and Reds who tried to interfere with their meeting.

The Communist Party, by extensive chalking, rallied the workers to demonstrate against the Fascists.

In due time the Fascists arrived to hold their meeting and found over 1,000 workers waiting for them.

About a hundred Fascists were marching behind a covered van, but before they could settle down to a meeting the mass of the workers moved towards them and the police wisely escorted them to a meeting-place about half a mile away.

An anti-Fascist meeting was started on the Broadway, but many workers followed the Fascists to their new meeting-place.

Here a relay of Fascist speakers, each one of whom lasted only a few minutes, attempted to address the meeting.

The workers drowned them by shouting :—

"Fascism means Mass Murder!"
"We don't want concentration camps."

The "Red Flag" and the "International were sung. Finally the Fascists, after half an hour of effort, abandoned the meeting and escorted by the police they marched away.

Deptford had not been stormed and the Fascists had been taught a lesson.

SOUTHAMPTON WELDERS STRIKE

While others were speaking from the platform, Kath left the room to address a crowd of 500 who had not been able to get into the hall, on account of the popularity of the event. When she returned to the packed hall for her moment to secure the members' nomination, the *Kentish Mercury* reporter wrote:

Mrs. Duncan (to give her her proper title – for, although her cropped hair and masculine attire give her, at first glance, a boyish appearance, she is a married woman) began her oration in soft, purring tones. Then she became dramatic. She told of her childhood and the struggle of her widowed mother in a tiny Scottish village, where she worked with her needle by the light of an oil lamp to provide her family with the bare necessities of life. She spoke of her dreams and aspirations, of the days when she graduated from the high school to her university and, lastly, of her entry into the teaching profession. "I joined the Independent Labour Party," she said, "and came to London in 1924. Then things began to develop, and I realized as an intellectual and responsible worker that I must not just let my heart and emotions run away with me, but I must understand the political situation... I joined the Communist party in 1926."

British Communist Party Leader Harry Pollitt

The reporter found her performance full of dramatic variety:

'Flinging her arms in the air, she raised her voice to a scream. Then she became soft and appealing to break out the next moment into a torrent of abuse against the capitalist system. She hammered on the table, clutched the air, and at last, discarding her jacket, rolled up the sleeves of her blouse above her elbows and continued. "The House of Commons," she declared with warmth, "is the most widely advertised, the most notorious and far flung platform in the world, whilst at the same time being the most corrupt platform in the world. And

145

I'm asking you to send your representative to the House of Commons in order to expose the corruption and the mockery of these false traitors and to enable us to go to the exchanges (job centers)*, the homes, and the factories to rally the workers in our determination to smash this Parliament and erect our own machinery."'*

'If you elect me as your spokesman to the House of Commons, I shall receive £400 a year, less whatever percentage of sacrifice is required as a member of Parliament. But the money will be handed over by me to the Communist Party, who will then give me what allowance they think necessary to keep me in health and strength; an allowance that would never exceed 34 shillings a week. In case any of you might think 34 a week is an objective which would mean a lot to a working-class woman, I might say I could have been given the opportunity to earn more than this in my present profession.'

Then, she spoke of the glowing and glorious picture of 150,000,000 men and women in Soviet Russia, in contrast to the paradise they had in capitalist Britain, a situation that would bring about the most savage attack against the working class known in our generation. "Every sacrifice we make," she declared, "will bring more complications for the system and greater hardships for ourselves."

"Victory is in sight!" she shouted with enthusiasm. "And the glorious day is dawning when the workers and this country will come into their own!"

The chairman of the meeting, in his eulogy of the candidate, said that he had known comrade Kath Duncan for some years as a teacher and a worker; and he could assure the audience that, although she had been described as a young girl with an Eton crop (at this point loud laughter filled the hall), she was a woman of rare and earnest determination.

The reporter of the *Kentish Mercury* went on to say that, in his speech, Comrade Sandy Duncan – the husband of Comrade Kath and the local organizer of the Communist Party, as well as the chairman of the Teachers' Defence Committee for London and a member of the executive committee of the East Lambeth – declared that teachers were part and parcel of the working class. The majority came from working-class homes, and it was only because they were an exceedingly corrupted section of the community that they had been paid a higher wage in order to ensure a contented teaching staff throughout the country. The bourgeois class realized that they had two very able agents in teachers and police officers; the latter to guard the right of private profit, and the teachers to instill into the minds of the children the imperialist dope. Now, however, they hoped that action in approaching strikes would be put forward and advocated by the rank and file of the National Union of Teachers. There were over 30 organizations – trade unions, one might call them – catering for the teachers, and it was these organizations on which one based class. They intended to call together the defense committees and also to organize meetings of parents, for the fight was not one confined to teachers. They realized that, in order to achieve victory, they must stand shoulder to shoulder with every other section of the working class that was being attacked. Sandy Duncan's speech was then followed on by a talk by Comrade Alf Lucas on the long history of the struggles of the Unemployed Workers' Movement in Greenwich and Deptford.

Only a matter of days after this meeting, the regional branch of the National Union of Teachers declared that the local community had raised the deposit Kath needed to stand; though, unfortunately, the number of people who donated money and attended her rallies was far greater than the number of those who actually bothered to vote for her. It seems that in South London, then as now, the voters prefer either not to vote or to elect party candidates who do nothing but take the money and only appear in public at election time; or perhaps, to take a slightly more positive view, it is the case that they refuse to vote for the best candidate – that is, the one most likely to address the issues and fight their corner – for fear that they will be corrupted by the system.

Kath fought an extremely high-profile campaign. At one public meeting, so the press report stated, '*After a number of supporters of Mrs. Kath Duncan, the Communist candidate, had interrupted a meeting of Mr. E. T. Palmer, the Labour nominee, at the Armada Hall, Greenwich, one of Mr. Palmer's supporters, yelled out, "I think our friends in the corner are chasing red herrings in skirts".*'

' "There are three candidates in this election," retorted Mr. Glynn Evans, Mr. Palmer's election agent, "Hume, Palmer, and Kath Bunkham." Mr. Evans then said that there was a cure for unemployment. A voice from the hall yelled, "Then why the hell hasn't the Labour Party used it during the last two-and-half years?" Mr. Palmer said that the Communists had given themselves away to him. "Don't be fooled by the nonsense that is being talked about at street corners by the Communist candidate," he said. "They gave the whole show away the other night. One of them asked me whether I believed in the ballot box; I said, "Yes, don't you?" He replied, "No." I asked him why they were putting up a candidate then, and he said, "Oh, that's just propaganda."'

Fundraising was set at 3,000 shillings, reaching 2,000 shillings after Mr. Richards – who until Kath's selection as a candidate had been a member of the General Council of the Labour Party of Greenwich and chairman of the East Greenwich branch of the local A.E. Union – stated at a public meeting that he was fed up with Labour. "Whilst I am a not a Communist," he said, "I am heart and soul for the worker, and that is why I am voting and working for Kath Duncan at the coming general election. I advise my fellow workers of Greenwich to do the same."

A few days later, the local press reported that a bodyguard of unemployed people had just left the Deptford Labour Exchange, accompanying Kath and her £150 deposit to Greenwich Town Hall to submit her application to stand. Once it had been submitted, Kath addressed the large crowd of some 400 people who had gathered outside from her box.

Kath left Sandy briefly in charge of her campaign in London when she returned to her hometown of Kilkcaldy, in Scotland, to help and support her fellow Communist candidate, William Gallagher. She was still loved and adored by the people. It was no surprise that Kath, as she had with Winston Churchill in Dundee, helped the Communists to win their first and only seat at Westminster. Sadly, however, Kath failed to get elected, losing her deposit in Greenwich.

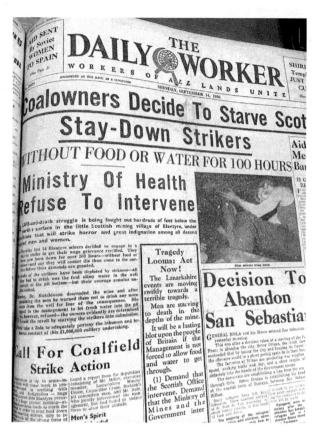

The Daily Worker newspaper front page, dated Monday, September 14, 1936, with headlines including "Coalowners Decide To Starve Scot Stay-Down Strikers", "Without Food Or Water For 100 Hours", "Ministry Of Health Refuse To Intervene", "Call For Coalfield Strike Action", "Tragedy Looms: Act Now!", "Decision To Abandon San Sebastian".

Deptford was shocked by the poor result. Kath secured just 2024 votes in a seat in which women outnumbered men on the electoral roll. Although angry and upset in equal measure, Kath just got on with the next campaign. She was still in high demand as a leader in the 'Friends of Russia' campaign and busy preparing for the next hunger marches and the next anti-fascist protest. Kath had done her best and more. Winning or losing would not change her commitment to activism or stop her relentless campaigning.

In May, 1933, welfare reforms were still a huge campaign issue, with abject poverty and hunger visible on almost every street corner. A march was organized to County Hall to present the latest petition against the means test and for increased support to those most in need. To maximize the numbers on the march, which had been banned by the police, the protestors, led by Kath, met in the morning, outside the Nynehead test center, as this was when the maximum number of unemployed were together in one place. Despite the ban on meetings and the planned march, Nynehead workers came out on strike and several hundred Deptford protestors linked up with fellow protestors from Camberwell and Brixton. Around 2500 in all, according to local reports, marched on County Hall.

At County Hall, some of the unemployed had secured places in the public gallery before the council meeting that they had come to lobby began. Kath Duncan and another activist, George Finch, lobbied the council officials for a deputation to be received. For nearly an hour, the council debated the Labour motion to receive Kath's deputation and then voted against it.

As the council refused the protestors the right to air their grievances, the unemployed protestors who had secured seating in the public gallery climbed over the barriers into the chamber, demanding that their concerns be heard, hurling their petition onto the platform at the chair of the committee. Council officials were called to keep order as fighting broke out, until the police rushed in and arrested the protestors. The success of the Labour Party in winning control of the London County Council, in 1934, was widely attributed to the anger that was generated by this failure to allow the unemployed to have a voice.

SIR OSWALD AND SIR MALCOLM

Jingoist Plots On Deptford ?

Last week we gave reports of Fascist activities in support of Tory electioneering in St. Pancras and Shoreditch. We now have reason to believe that there is an understanding between Mosley and Sir Malcolm Campbell, the Tory candidate for Deptford. Mosley is holding a meeting at Greenwich Baths or the eve of the poll, and there is little doubt that his jingoist propaganda will find a sympathetic echo in the heart of the Tory speedace whose slogan is "Country first—always."

The Woolwich Sub-District of the C.P. has called on all the workers in Deptford, Greenwich, Lewisham, and Woolwich to rally in opposition.

Kee
Off

Attempts
Fascists t
in schoc
resisted b
authoriti
Such
made a
Green, v
class de
childrer
Socialis
protect
danger
Fascist

The Scottish hunger marchers had arrived in London at the same time as the London County Council elections. In Deptford – thanks to Kath, the Communist Party, and the National Union of Unemployed Workers' Movement – local interest in the election was far greater than it had been in 1931. The party believed that it could win elections and take control of the deeply unpopular Public Assistance committee of London.

As Kath Duncan was the best-known communist in the country and, by all accounts, the voice of the people of Deptford, she was to stand as the party candidate in the council elections, together with Vic Parker. The party felt it had a clear-cut policy for alleviating the unemployment problem, at its source, by providing work for nearly a quarter of a million people. They put forward a well-thought-out policy agenda to tackle slum housing issues, by building 250,000 new council homes, a quite extraordinary proposal and radical for the time. And this proposal would later be a keystone policy of Clement Attlee's Labour Party, whose success at the 1945 General Elections inaugurated the golden years of the Labour movement in power. Both Labour and the Conservatives are proposing this very policy today, in 2018.

The Communist Party's manifesto also put forward proposals to repair and rebuild bridges and congested roads and crossings, supply piped water to every house without it, and to strengthen the riverbanks to improve flood defenses, as well as to construct a new electric railway for East London. Kath Duncan could not have been more pleased to be able to stand on such a platform, which also promised to restore the 10% unemployed benefit cuts and abolish the means test, a bit like today's universal credit.

The *Kentish Mercury* wrote of Kath's campaign, '*Comrade Kath Duncan, an eloquent speaker with a superabundance of force and emotion, is fighting her campaign with her usual vitality.*'

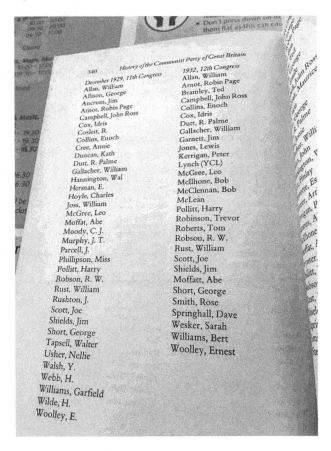

340   *History of the Communist Party of Great Britain*

December 1929, 11th Congress

Allan, William
Allison, George
Ancrum, Jim
Arnot, Robin Page
Campbell, John Ross
Cox, Idris
Coslett, R.
Collins, Enoch
Cree, Annie
Duncan, Kath
Dutt, R. Palme
Gallacher, William
Hannington, Wal
Herman, E.
Hoyle, Charles
Joss, William
McGree, Leo
Moffat, Abe
Moody, C. J.
Murphy, J. T.
Parcell, J.
Phillipson, Miss
Pollitt, Harry
Robson, R. W.
Rust, William
Rushton, J.
Scott, Joe
Shields, Jim
Short, George
Tapsell, Walter
Usher, Nellie
Walsh, Y.
Webb, H.
Williams, Garfield
Wilde, H.
Woolley, E.

1932, 12th Congress

Allan, William
Arnot, Robin Page
Bramley, Ted
Campbell, John Ross
Collins, Enoch
Cox, Idris
Dutt, R. Palme
Gallacher, William
Garnett, Jim
Jones, Lewis
Kerrigan, Peter
Lynch (YCL)
McGree, Leo
McIlhone, Bob
McClennan, Bob
McLean
Pollitt, Harry
Robinson, Trevor
Roberts, Tom
Robson, R. W.
Rust, William
Scott, Joe
Shields, Jim
Moffatt, Abe
Short, George
Smith, Rose
Springhall, Dave
Wesker, Sarah
Williams, Bert
Woolley, Ernest

One report makes much of Kath's popularity and of the love and respect that were shown to her even by those whom she had come to blows with over the years. A bouquet of red carnations arrived at her campaign office on Tanners Hill, in Deptford, with best wishes and good luck from the boys of Surrey Commercial Dock, a kind gesture from the very same dockers who had previously thrown red ochre over her.

Although the voter turnout (50%) was much higher than in the previous election (28%), it was Labour that gained the seats, with Kath polling 1387 votes and Vic Parker 1177. Vic was reported as saying, 'If we could have gone on the size and enthusiasm of our meetings, and the verbal assurances of the folks we canvassed, we should have been in the top poll.'

But sadly, despite two candidates and a policy agenda that would have transformed the lives of the poor in Deptford, it was not to be. People would continue to vote Labour, regardless of the poor quality of the candidates, and ignore exceptional people, such as the recent Lewisham People Before Profit candidates in Deptford, years after Kath Duncan had left the scene; and thus would cut off their noses to spite their faces, as the old saying goes.

The campaign that Kath had fought so hard, the fantastic policy manifesto they had all fought for, and the clear public support – even though the voters eventually failed to follow through at the ballot box – did ensure that the next unemployment demonstration to County Hall did not lead to its leaders being arrested and jailed again. This time, a warm welcome would be the order of the day, and £350,000 would be found to fund unemployment relief in London, a staggering sum of money for the time.

Image of Kath Duncan, in the1930s

Losing elections was not something that troubled Kath all that much. She saw the wider picture and felt that putting up solutions and standing for what she believed in, from a principled position, made her politics all the stronger. However, I suspect that Mama and Sandy took a different point of view, and many still ask why Deptford never elected Kath to public office. Would winning a seat on the Borough Council have been a more likely option? No one in Deptford's history has done as much as Kath did for the community she lived in, or paid such a high price. It's almost as if the people did not vote for her because they did not want to view her as just another politician and wanted to keep 'our Kath' as she was.

The 1930s were a constant onslaught of attacks on the poorest and most vulnerable in society, and after her first period in jail, Kath had lost her job as a teacher. On her release from jail, her union and the Communist Party had mobilized and collected thousands of signatures to get the original decision overturned. They were successful, but only in the short term.

A conservative MP, Captain Todd, raised her case in the House of Commons, asking the Secretary to the Board of Education whether he was aware that Mrs. Kath Duncan, a London County Council school teacher, having been sentenced to 12 months' imprisonment for incitement, had only been cautioned by the London County Council education committee and was now again teaching in a London School. He inquired also that her husband, Mr. A.K. Duncan, having been fined in 1932 for taking part in a riot, was also only cautioned by London County Council and was, at present, teaching in a grant-aided school. He also asked whether steps would be taken to ensure that teachers convicted of offences of this nature were not allowed to teach British children.

Mr. Ramsbottom replied that Mrs. Duncan was charged with being a disturber of the peace and an inciter of others to commit crimes. She was ordered by the magistrate to find a surety of £50 to keep the peace for six months or go to prison. She chose the latter course. She had not, in fact, been employed by the London County Council since September last. Mrs. Kath Duncan was also fined £5 for obstructing a police officer in the execution of his duty. The Board of Education had been made aware of these two cases and were considering what further action could or ought to be taken in regard to them, under their regulations.

"The Board's regulations," added Mr Ramsbottom, "state clearly that if a teacher is convicted of a criminal offence, the facts must be at once reported to the Board. And the case, therefore, of Mrs. Duncan should have been reported. I understand that it was through inadvertence that this was not done, and that steps have been taken to ensure strict compliances with the regulations for the future. In Mrs. Duncan's case, the Court did not proceed to a conviction and there was, therefore, no similar obligation on the London County Council to report the fact."

Captain Todd replied, "Is my Honorable Friend aware that in their issue of February 4th, the *Daily Worker* published an article suggesting that they had been able to intimidate the Education Committee of the London County Council and prevent them acting against these teachers? And does he not consider that action should be taken to prevent teachers with such a close connection with international atheism and communism from teaching British children?"

Mr. Ramsbottom responded, "In reply to the first part of the supplementary question, I am aware of the facts stated. Regarding the second part of the question, it would be unwise to say anything to prejudice the position in view of the investigation which is to take place."

Mr. Maxton, MP, asked whether the Honorable Gentleman was aware that both these teachers had very excellent records as members of the teaching profession, and if he would resist the suggestion that teachers should be subjected to prosecution for holding special political views.

Mr. Ramsbottom replied: "The teaching record of these two persons is, I understand, satisfactory."

This debate about Kath Duncan was purely politically motivated. Kath Duncan's record as an inspired and brilliant teacher was well-known. She taught children that she truly cared about, and she loved her profession with every beat of her heart. Her activism and politics were kept away from her school and classroom. Sadly, after this House of Common's interaction, she would never teach again. Sandy, who had been so successful as a teacher of sport that the school's trophy cabinet was full, would be allowed to continue to be the breadwinner for the household, while Kath could become a full-time activist.

Many believe that another reason this case was brought to the House of Commons was to embarrass Winston Churchill. Kath had been a close friend of Winston Churchill's wife, and they had both been suffragettes together with a common bond, in the early 1900s. They both shared a common and very negative view of the 'vulgar' Tories. Kath had been a crucial member of Churchill's campaign team that secured his election success in the Dundee by-election of 1917; and she had also been a guest at his wedding, in 1908. This debate on Kath's teaching was a cheap shot that would probably not have registered outside the political bubble of Westminster if the friendship had not been widely known about but kept secret.

After her general election campaign of 1931, Kath Duncan would no longer stand for or hold any position within the Communist Party, even though she was the Party's most capable advocate. She was extremely popular, and she was the reason that many joined the Party at a time when many communists who were members of the union movement were told they had to support the Labour Party and not the communists. Many communists did indeed join the Labour movement, and yet many, against party orders, would rally to Kath's call.

Women had real issues with the Party, and Kath travelled as far as Wales to address Welsh women's concerns about the way they felt the Party had failed them after the successes of the suffragette movement and its activism. Kath believed strongly in equality, social justice, and civil rights, and she was a strong advocate within the Party to build alliances across the union and Labour movement. With no job since 1933, Kath was in a stronger position, as Sandy was still teaching and bringing home a decent wage, for the time being. The need for her activism was relentless, and yet the sparkle of the Communist Party was waning and many, such as her great friend Fred Copeman, wondered why she would remain so steadfastly loyal to the flag.

In September, 1936, Kath would be involved in a battle that would ensure she would never again be permitted to stand as a Communist Party candidate or for a position within the Party. The local gas company, South Met, which had 1.5 million customers, was looking to change the way it charged for gas. Having a monopoly over an area of 52 square miles, they could almost do and charge what they liked. Under the new scale of charges that they were proposing, the tariff increased for the poorest consumers but decreased for the big consumers. The increase to the poorest was approximately 20%. The real beneficiaries were shopkeepers, better-off customers, and local councils who, for example, ran the street lights. One councilor in Camberwell stated to the local press at the time: "The gas company is attempting to bribe the large consumers at the expense of the smaller consumer. A company which has made the profits that it has made can afford to pay its own bribes."

Kath was at the forefront of the protest movement across South London that was up and running within a week of the new charges being in place. Deptford Borough Council, after lobbying, passed a resolution of 'emphatic protest' and a meeting was called and took place on 29 September, at Deptford Town Hall.

With the mayor in the chair, the crowd that turned up was so large that speeches had to be relayed onto the streets outside. So great was the public outrage that, on 30 September, at a private meeting in Deptford Town Hall, a joint committee was formed in which were all the area's MPs, all the local London County Council members, all the mayors from the whole of South London, and Kath, because of her importance to Deptford.

The very next day, on 1 October, Kath led a march of 2,000 Deptford residents on the gas company's offices on the Old Kent Road. By the time they had arrived at the gas company, the crowd had grown to 30,000 and was blocking the roads, and the police were called to divert the traffic. This official group was in addition to the mass campaign that was being built by Kath and others at street level, with street meetings and rallies being held across South London by the Labour Party, Communist Party, and associations of rate payers and tenants. This was all supported with a letter and postcard campaign directed at elected politicians, the King, and the Prime Minister. The London County Council proposed special legislation to prevent such action by private gas companies from happening in the future. The joint committee urged the Board of Trade to intervene.

On 7 October, a women's march was organized from Deptford Broadway at midday, with women pushing prams and carrying banners of protest. The Women's Co-op and Women's Guild, not known for their outspokenness, were just two of the women's groups that took part. One woman played the mouth organ as they sang the songs of the day on their march to the Old Kent Road. The image of Kath giving an impassioned speech to the huge crowd that eventually assembled adorned the front page of the *South London Press*.

Many people started to think of how best they could break the charges. Some thought that switching to electricity was the best solution, although it was costly. Others took more direct action by boycotting their gas stoves and raking out their old oil-filled or wood-burning stoves. For days, the only talk was about how different it was cooking without gas. Their spirit may not have bankrupted the gas company, but the people of Deptford would not give it one penny more.

On 13 October, another protest was organized and led by MPs, London County Council members, and mayors across South London, including Deptford's own mayor. The meeting point was Camberwell Library, a much shorter walk to the gasworks than the usual setting off point on Deptford Broadway – a place steeped in the history of working-class struggle and protest.

The gas company was eventually forced to scrap the unfair tariff system by the biggest and most united expression of the will of the people that had yet been seen in South London. And the initiative came from Deptford. The power of a great capitalist monopoly was temporarily broken by working people. Such a protest would not be seen again in this area until the New Crossfire Protests in South London in the 1970s, and the hugely successful 'Save Lewisham Hospital' campaign that, at its start, would be powered by another Deptford-driven party, Lewisham People Before Profit.

The rise of fascism, which saw Sir Oswald Mosley's Blackshirts marching on the streets of Britain, gave the Communist Party another full-on campaign to fight. Whilst many thought they would just go away if they were ignored, the Communist Party mobilized huge numbers in opposition, collecting signatures on petitions to ban its marches, and at every opportunity, being present to challenge its rhetoric. This came at a huge cost to the Party; hardly a week passed without a member of the Communist Party being arrested, charged, fined, and often jailed for standing up to the fascists, and yet very few fascists would be dealt with by the state with the harshness that the state lavished on the communists.

On 4 October, 1936, one of the most famous battles in British history took place on Cable Street, East London. For weeks prior to it, Oswald Mosley had been making plans to march his Blackshirts through the streets of East London, and 100,000 people had signed petitions calling for the march to be stopped. The tension in East London was palpable, and the East London branch of the Communist Party, led by Phil Piratin, organized and mobilized huge numbers of communists and other people from across London who were opposed to fascism to come and stand with the people of Cable Street to ensure the Blackshirts would not pass. Kath, having been an activist in Hackney for seven years before moving to Deptford, welcomed the chance to visit old friends and mobilized her own Deptford army to support Phil and her fellow comrades on the frontline.

Kath was justly proud of the fact that the Blackshirts never succeeded in marching down Cable Street that day. However, whilst the awareness of the battle would help put a stop to the rise of Sir Oswald's political ambition, modern history has chosen to rob the Communist Party of the credit it deserves for its relentless activism in opposing him and the terrible price it paid; so many of its members were jailed, with appalling consequences for their lives and well-being.

This was another great battle that had kept Kath firmly in the Communist Party's ranks; but, increasingly, she felt that the work and the punishment were being carried on the shoulders of its activists and not its leadership.

The Party was furious about Kath Duncan's role in the protests against the gas company. The Party was not keen to share the campaign with such an inclusive activist as Kath. They felt that the revolution would come about by the masses rebelling against the appalling injustice they endured, while Kath's position was always that the revolution would only come about by a united alliance of the Left, including the union movement and the Labour Party.

As Sandy and Kath were both active union members, it was tough when most unions were passing motions banning their members from joining the Communist Party and certainly from taking any part in their campaigns. Kath was told she would no longer be permitted to stand for any public office or for the Party again. Fred Copeman and others were appalled and would write later that this was a turning point which led them to feel that they did not wish to remain within the Communist Party any longer.

Fred would later state that the final straw for him was when he was sitting in his office one day and a leading member of the Party submitted a tailor's receipt for the purchase of a suit, in Liverpool, priced at £2.10 that had clearly been altered to read £3.10. Fred at once highlighted his concern that the receipt had been altered, only for the Party official to say, "I will have to take this up with Harry Pollitt," (leader of the British Communist Party). Fred asked him why that would be necessary, and he replied, "Because you've changed the amount on the receipt." In the following minutes, events moved very fast. Fred lost his temper and let his boxing skills take over. He launched a punch and knocked the official out cold. As he came to, he yelled out, "Murder! Help!" Fred went straight to the office of Harry Pollitt, on King Street, and was assured by Harry not to worry. "Take no notice," he said.

The next morning, Fred again met with Harry in the churchyard close to the office on King Street. Harry suggested that Fred had been working too hard and needed to rest... permanently. Fred had been expecting him to pass over the whole event as an incident of no great consequence, but he had clearly rethought his stance overnight. Fred Copeman, one of the greatest Communist Party activists and leaders of the age, was no longer welcome as a party member.

This decision left Fred very depressed. He returned to his other job as a steel erecting foreman and tried to forget the whole affair. He discussed the issue with his friend and fellow communist activist Charlotte Haldane, who assured him that, in her opinion, there was nothing in it; that politics was not really Fred's line, as he was far too sentimental; that politics was a harsh business; and that, by now, he should be well aware that things necessary for a good military commander did not always make a successful politician.

Kath and Sandy Duncan, however, were not prepared to let it go and were furious. Fred was their closest comrade, and there could never be a finer man. Kath stormed into Harry's office, demanding an apology for Fred, only for Harry to say that this was not the first time that Fred had flown off the handle and knocked someone out. Harry continued, "Fred has become a pretty awkward cuss to work with, and it was thought best to allow him to quietly pass on."

Many leading Party activists, like Fred, had joined specifically because of Kath and probably would have followed her to the moon and back. Kath accepted that this was the way things were. Fred concentrated on his work within the Constructional Engineering Union and would later write that what he did in hitting a man and knocking him out cold was clearly not acceptable. The party had lost one of its true heroes, and looking back today, this was probably the point at which Kath felt that the Labour Party, under its then leadership, was probably more in tune with her ideas of revolution.

In July, 1934, reports arrived in Deptford that the fascist Blackshirts had attempted to hold their first meeting in Kirkcaldy, Kath's hometown, only for her comrades and friends to chase them out of town. Before the fascists had arrived, the Communist Party had held a meeting and explained why the Blackshirts should not be allowed a hearing. Just then, the crowd ran towards the fascists, seized the platform, and smashed it. The local newspapers reported that they '...smashed their platform to smithereens and tore up their papers.'

A large anti-fascist meeting was then held. Members of the Labour Party and other organizations took part in the anti-fascist demonstration; and the basis for a united front against fascism and war had been laid in Kirkcaldy, the only place in the country that, in 1931, sent a Communist MP to Westminster. These were two aspects of Kath's hometown that would make her and her household immensely proud.

On 28 November, 1937, Rose Cohen, one of Kath's earliest comrades, was executed in Russia as a spy. The two women had met and campaigned together from 1924. Cohen had been given a job at the Soviet embassy in 1925, the same year she had met David Petrovsky, whom she would marry in 1929 and have a son with. Like many of Kath's circle, she was not only a great intellectual, as was her sister Nellie, but was also a great beauty. Communist Party leader, Harry Pollitt, would joke about the huge number of times she had declined his advances. One of the key women who had introduced Kath to the Communist Party, and to her husband, Cohen was arrested in March, 1937, and then expelled from the Russian Communist Party. On 13 August, Cohen herself was arrested in Moscow and charged as a spy. She denied all the charges and pleaded her innocence, right up to her untimely death.

In April, 1938, the British government confirmed that Rose had never been a spy and, despite living the last years of her life in Russia, had never given up her British citizenship. It would take until 1956, after the 20th congress of the Communist Party of the Soviet Union, for her son, Alexey D. Petrovsky, to be able to file an appeal to review her case. And on 8 August, 1956, the Military Collegium of the USSR Supreme Court invalidated the ruling that had been made against Cohen on 28 November, 1937. All charges were dropped, and the case was dismissed for lack of corpus delicti – in other words, a lack of fundamental evidence. Cohen was posthumously recognized as a victim of political repression, sadly two years after Kath Duncan's death.

In 1936, the year before her execution, Kath had met Rose again, when she was on a visit to London. At this time, she was working for the *Moscow Daily News* and had been so highly thought of and trusted as a communist that she had been trusted to travel extensively to Lithuania, Estonia, Latvia, Turkey, France, Norway, and Sweden on secret state missions. This entailed delivering letters and transferring funds to local communist parties. The silence of the Communist Party leadership on the matter of her being a spy was, therefore, appallingly disloyal, as anyone who had known the Cohen sisters would be aware that the charges could not be true. Kath was furious that, when both Harry Pollitt and Willie Gallacher had appealed to the secretary general of the Executive Committee of Communist International, George Dimitrov, they had simple accepted being told, 'Do not interfere'. With the party sitting on its hands, it was only others on the left, led by Maurice Reckitt, who would protest loudly and by letter make the point that it was all a terrible mistake; a mistake which could have been avoided if the British government had intervened sooner.

The Party's position on the expected outbreak of World War II, and the fact that Kath's husband had been ejected from the Communist Party because he had been a Young Conservative for four weeks as a teenager, probably weighed heavily on Kath's mind. This, together with Fred's reports from the frontline of the Spanish Civil War, helped to undermine her feelings of loyalty to the Party. The Communist Party had done nothing when she had been jailed twice, despite her gaining huge goodwill for the Party cause. Although, in 1954, upon her death, they were quick to heap praise on her, the reality is that she probably would have accepted Clement Attlee's invitation to stand as a Labour candidate in the 1945 general election, if it had not been for her poor health.

Clement Attlee had become friends with Fred Copeman, and it was through this friendship that Clement Attlee would be a regular visitor to Kath's new home on Waller Road, where they got on extremely well. Kath was only too aware of her own failing health. She was too weak to seek membership of the Labour Party, although she had joined the Independent Labour Party long ago, when she was a young girl. Although she could not stand for parliament, she did pledge, come what may, that she would do what she could to help Attlee win the 1945 election. Despite being in great pain and poor health, she honored that pledge, working in the Deptford parliamentary campaign office, addressing envelopes with her crippled hands. People dropped by to pledge support or offer help, as they had always done in the past for Kath and Sandy. The Labour agent and candidate were glad to benefit from her extensive knowledge of the borough; its issues and its people.

Chapter Nine
¡Viva la República!
The Spanish Civil War

'Viva la República!' might have brought joy to the left in London, but war was increasingly all too common across Europe. Franco's revolution was not one that they would welcome, as many of them would find themselves either on the frontline of an ill-equipped army of idealists or at home, reading the telegrams of lost comrades killed in this cruel war.

The Spanish Civil War of 1936 was a struggle between a democratically elected socialist government and its people against fascism. The generals, under Franco, had risen in a military coup to overthrow the government, which had the support of Italy and Germany. The rest of Europe, including Britain, kept quiet and stayed away. This left the people very much on their own to rise and fight to defend their fledgling democracy. Whilst Italy and Germany stood against Franco's international armed rebels, the mass media just ran a negative campaign against the Spanish government. The communists and the working-class and union movements sent ships loaded with food and medical supplies.

Deptford had its own Spanish aid committee, which, with Kath in full form, raise hundreds of pounds door-to-door to buy an ambulance, which was handed over by Leah Manning to the Spanish embassy at a garden fete in the grounds of Goldsmith College. Kath, as the reports of the day state, threw herself with all her characteristic energy into the fundraising campaign.

Kath also had an important role in interviewing those who wished to go and fight. Around 500 from Deptford would go. After selling her copies of the *Daily Worker* on a Saturday afternoon and having held a meeting from her box on Deptford

Broadway in the evening, as she did every Saturday, she would be up early Sunday morning calling door-to-door for the envelopes left the day before for money for Spain. She would relentlessly address as many meetings and rallies as she could get to in a day and march on every protest in Central London for the cause. This was very much Kath's war.

During the First World War, she had seen the massive loss of life and the impact on families and friends within her community. However, her father had died when she was just 5-years-old, so the impact of war was not directly felt in the Duncan household. Nevertheless, Kath and Sandy would see not just hundreds of their comrades sent to war, but the family's closest friend, Fred Copeman, who was like a brother to them, sent to fight on the frontline.

Fred was determined, before setting off to fight in Spain, that he would have the courage to speak to a young woman that had caught his attention at the Deptford branch of the Young Communists League. Fred had fallen for a young student who seemed to hold the position of secretary and who was usually at the door, collecting the money. Fred chose to discuss his feelings, which had become a bit of a joke in the Duncan household, with Sandy. With Mama also keeping a close eye out for Fred, Sandy spoke with the young student, whose name was Kitty, and pleaded the case of a young man who had nobody to go to the pictures with. It was a good match. Kitty was part of a large socialist family whose mother and father helped to run the Lewisham Socialist Sunday School while still raising their own children as atheists. Kitty would eventually become Fred's wife, and they became engaged just before he set off for Spain.

A reader has sent the "Daily Worker" this photo of Felicia Browne, London Communist, who has been killed fighting for the Government in Spain.

Kath, as always, put a bright face on and decided that, whilst she could not personally go to Spain (women were forbidden), she could help in other ways. Kitty came to stay at 68 Ommaney Road and Kath would be in Deptford and on King Street – the main departure points for recruits – interviewing the men wanting to fight.

With Fred so far away at war, the stories that were coming back were a constant cause of concern. Why was the Russian government not supplying proper arms? Why were the world's leaders and governments so indifferent to the democratically elected socialist Spanish government?

Whilst men were supposedly carefully selected to fight, many had never even held a gun. Although women were forbidden to fight, one of the first deaths reported from the frontline was of Kath's friend, Felicia Browne, who disguised herself as a boy to fight for the government in Spain, only to pay the ultimate price. Felicia Browne was the first British casualty of the war and was shot whilst carrying a wounded comrade on the Aragon front, in Northeast Spain, while they were on a night patrol to search out weapons and ammunition. Felicia was a London-based artist and activist who thought that she was doing the right thing by going to Spain.

When the Spanish Civil War broke out, Fred wrote that he was increasingly moving away from the Communist Party and falling out of love with it, choosing instead to spend more time with the Labour movement. During the Spanish Civil War, on a visit from Clement Attlee – a brigade was named after him – Fred became a close friend who would introduce him to Kath and Sandy. They would, likewise, come to have huge respect for Attlee and spend many long hours discussing politics in London.

Every week, Fred would be meeting with Kath and Sandy, and it was impossible not to talk politics. On this particular Saturday, Fred got into a conversation with a young Scottish nurse who was staying with Kath and Sandy and was describing the attitude of the London County Council to the nurses. The anomaly of these girls, many of them from good families, giving their lives to nurse sick people in return for an inadequate wage, and often in disgusting living conditions, started Fred thinking. He decided he must go to Spain; and within three days, he arrived at the Spanish border, fueled with idealism and a belief he would be fighting for freedom.

1930 to 1936 had seen the rapid rise of totalitarian governments across Europe, with the odd success, such as France's Front Populaire and the overthrow of the Spanish monarchy. The new Spanish Republican government, established in April, 1931, was made up of intellectuals with the support and solidarity of the Labour union movement. The initial reaction from the ordinary Spanish population was one of support and interest, which helped to quickly suppress the first rebellion in 1932, led by General San Juro, allowing the government to show strength and ability.

The first line of policy for the new government was to write a constitution, declaring Spain a worker's republic of all classes and promising labor a share in the rewards of industry. In addition, all women were given the vote and primary education for every child became compulsory and free.

Despite being a country in which religion played such a powerful role in all aspects of society, the government separated the state from the church. Illegitimacy was abolished and divorce was made possible. Such a radical and progressive agenda would not be easy to implement, and the government was quickly defeated by an alliance on the right with a general suppression of socialist leaders and radical thoughts until the start of 1936.

The 1936 Spanish general election returned the parties of the Left Alliance and Popular Front back into power, with 4,838,449 votes, while the right received 3,996,931. As the government set out to reactivate the police agenda of 1931, an uprising was launched and led by General Francisco Franco. When Lieutenant Castillo of the assault police, and a popular left leader, was assassinated, the left retaliated by assassinating Signor Calvo Sotello, whom the right had in mind to lead them.

General Franco, the then governor of the Canary Islands, flew to Morocco and – with the support of Italy, Moorish troops, and the French Foreign Legion – broke the blockade at Gibraltar and captured the city of Seville. Fred wrote, '*In civil war one must expect the bloodiest of fighting, and no doubt atrocities were committed by both sides.*'

The reports from the *Times* led to increasing numbers of people from across the world heading for Spain, and the International Brigade had a hugely important moral effect on Spain's republican forces.

By January, 1937, some 27,000 men would be fighting in the Brigade, with 800 from Britain alone. The Communist Party's headquarters at King Street made all the arrangements, with Kath, Sandy, and Kitty doing their best to ensure that the send-off for Fred and his team would be one of smiles and solidarity, not tears.

170

On 26 November, 1936, Fred led a small party of men on a boat train to Paris and then on, through the night, to Perpignan, a town in the southwest corner of France. Fred was not alone. On his arrival, some 300 fellow Britons were also in town there, the trooped being commanded by a man named Shapayev, who would later become better known as General Tito.

In the late evening of the third day, packed into lorries, the group headed out over the stunning landscape of the Pyrenees to reach Figueras, the meeting base for all volunteers just inside the Spanish border.

On his arrival at the Spanish base, Fred would write home, *'I was elected to take charge of the British contingent of some 400 men and lead them through Barcelona to Albacete, General Franco's hometown, a distance of 250 miles. The charming backdrop of whitewashed villages did not reflect the newspaper reports and stories that are reported at home.'*

The calm, however, would be short-lived, as the fascists got wind that they were based at Albacete. Aerial bombing would become a regular event whilst the 16th British Battalion was being formed. The commander was Wilfred McCartney, a progressive journalist who wrote *Walls have Mouths*. His second-in-command, Tom Wintringham, was a member of a well-known liberal family and a military correspondent for the *Daily Worker*. The Communist Party was officially represented by Douglas 'Dave' Springhall and Peter Kerrigan as political commissars, as most of the volunteers now were members of the Communist Party.

Fred's issues with the Communist Party, who had not been enthusiastic about his decision to fight in Spain, would lead to more than one difficult situation. This growing mistrust on both sides, and Fred's later criticism of the Communist Party, is probably the reason why his activism, party work, and importance during the Spanish Civil War have been largely ignored by modern-day writers. If you are recording history, it must be correct, even if you have issues with those who are a part of it. To erase them, as many have done to Fred Copeman, is to distort the reality and lose the argument, as your story becomes one about those who have not been ignored, rather than the true story of heroism, bravery, and solidarity.

Fred wrote that, throughout his experience with the Party, so long as there was a job to be done which agreed with the principles of the working-class movement, he felt enthusiasm for it. However, continuously cutting across this feeling was an unhappiness caused by what he saw as the attitude of the party to individual problems, with its ruthless opposition to a contrary point of view. This was not helped by the poor quality of the arms they had to fight with and constant Party political dogma.

Fred was able to write home to Kath and Kitty, reporting the story of their friend, George Bright. George was 60 years old and had arrived to help with carpentry, being too old to fight. Even though people volunteered, the frontline was selective about who was able to fight and many arguments would break out over those who had lied about their age. Fred was speaking to George, when he was tragically shot in the head and killed instantly. His union card fluttered out as he fell. ' *"Aww," I thought, "what an awful thing it was that he, at his age, should be here, and yet I am certain he would not have wished for any other end."* '

As the battle carried on and calls came of the dead and wounded, Fred was hit in the head. He said it was a curious feeling, rather like receiving morphia. *'Everything went warm and I felt sleepy. All that I looked at had a red tinge about it, and yet I could still see to move around. By this point, the pain in my head had gone and I almost forgot that the bullet was very much in my head. Heading back to the hospital tent, I felt like half my head had been blown off, but luckily my injuries were minor; many would not see another sunrise.'*

It was not long before Fred would be back on the frontline and writing home about a great battle on the Cordova front, led by Jock Cunningham, who, under intense attack from the Moors, held the hilltop through the courage and tenacity of a group of British volunteers who scraped with their fingers to produce cover and used dead bodies as breastwork. Unskilled in the art of war and under-equipped – and with the sound of singing *The Internationale* in their lungs – they held and won through, holding and securing this position until the end of the war.

As darkness fell, the hospital was like a morgue, with many dead; 630 men had fought that day and less than 80 had escaped unharmed. Fred was appointed battalion commander, which caused some friction because of his refusal to accept the right of political commissars to influence military organizations and discipline. One action had brought a spate of demands for harsher punishment of those who had left the line, in part due to the terribly low morale bought on by the lack of weapons and ammunition and access to a decent meal. Fred agreed that there should be punishment, but within reason and commensurate with the crime, if a crime could be proven, bearing in mind that all the men had been wounded at least once and were fighting for the cause without pay or favor.

Kath was feeling the pressure, aware that Fred was taking huge risks and that, in a war situation, being rebellious could see him shot. The Party in London was desperate for Kath to use her influence to make Fred conform.

Fred had a long talk with his best comrade, Tappy (Wally Tapsell), during the last days, and it was agreed that Fred would return home, ostensibly to obtain more recruits, but in reality to be available for the inevitable political fight that was bound to take place.

The war had taken on a totally different perspective from how it had begun. The fight for the republican government was now more about a struggle over party ideology and political control. Very few of the original volunteers could be expected to give their whole-hearted support in these circumstances, though, due to the loss of so many comrades. Fred felt bound to continue the struggle. '*I saw no reason why indiscriminate shooting of volunteers should be permitted. Comrade Tappy, the Battalion's political commissar, felt the same way; the fight between the men and the Party would have to be settled.*'

Upon Fred's safe return to London, the relieved and ecstatic Kath, Kitty, and Sandy were at the station to collect him and take him home to Ommaney Road, Mama's great home cooking, and a hot kitchen bath.

For the next few days, Fred was busy addressing meetings across the country and raising another 350 volunteers who would later return with him and Tappy to Spain. One morning, a telephone call summoned Fred to the Communist Party office in King Street. Tappy told Fred that things were about to erupt, and he thought Fred should be there. Despite not having received any invitation from Harry Pollitt, leader of the Party, on entering Harry's office, Fred was greeted by the Party's political bureau, with Kerrigan, Rust, Springhall, Williams, George Aitken, Tappy, and Jock Cunningham sitting around a large table in a room, clouded in tobacco smoke. Jock made a case for a change in attitude to the rank and file of the battalion, for the withdrawal of the older volunteers, and for political education in conformity with the principles for which these men had gone to put down their lives for Spain. The counter argument, which emerged through shouting and threatening, was for stricter communist control. For over an hour, Jock held to his simple, sincere attempt to face up to the sneers and criticisms of people who had seldom had to risk their own hides, if at all, during the whole of the Spanish Civil War. Only a few weeks before, Jock had been featured in the *Daily Worker* as the British Lenin; now, he was having to face insinuations which amounted to nothing less than hints of fascist tendencies and, in one case, temporary insanity.

It was shocking for Fred to witness this and to see Jock break down. The cynical disregard for all that he had done for the Party and the cause – coupled with the self-satisfied claims of intellectuals and the unconcerned counting of causalities – was too much. Comrade Tappy entered the fray at this point, quietly, with a logical contribution that affected everyone in the room:

The political essence of all that has been spoken here is expressed in the bodies of 500–600 British comrades lying dead in Spain. Our responsibility is to them and not to ourselves. If we love the Party, we can do no less than ensure the safety of those that remain. If we still believe in the aims of the republican government, we must add to the number of our volunteers. Someone here has a job in Spain. We should be deciding who it is. Cunningham is a fine soldier, and I will take no part in any attempt to ridicule his sacrifice and efforts.

Harry Pollitt held up the meeting briefly to take a call and Fred looked around the room. He had always hated the regimental structure of political meetings, and even more so when they took on the complexion this meeting was taking.

Jock had clearly decided that he was in the wrong camp. He would hate everyone in that room from then on, and Fred just hoped that he was not included.

Fred told Kath he was not sure whether the occasion was big enough to make it one of open rebellion against the Party leadership, but he sided with Comrade Tappy; after all, whatever happened here, the final decision would be made on Spanish soil. Fred had a sense of duty and sense of loyalty to those lost and the many still left fighting on the frontline. He had picked up excitement from the new volunteers, although there was no shortage of people returning from Spain with horror stories to tell and a political party to undermine.

The political bureau agreed that Tappy and Fred would return to Spain, at once, with the maximum number of new recruits, and that the leaders of the political commissariat, except for Rust, would remain in England.

Harry Pollitt finished the meeting saying, "Only two people in this meeting have shown an impartial attitude to the problems being debated, Fred Copeman and Wally Tapsell (Tappy). We are lucky to have such comrades."

Fred and Tappy left the room to get ready for Spain. Kitty was far from happy that Fred, having been shot twice in Spain – and with his consistently critical comments and concern about every aspect of the way the war was going – would even consider going back to fight, especially after the way Jock had treated him. Kath was confused by the whole affair, her love for the Party cause balanced against the love of a comrade. After Sandy, her friend Fred was the most important man in her life and she cared for him hugely. Harry Pollitt's praise for Fred was unexpected and opened her mind to other thoughts. This was a party leader who had no problem supporting volunteers being shot for leaving the frontline, in many cases because they simply had nothing to fight with. Kath had expected Fred's return to be exactly that, his return to safety and helping her in the daily struggle of holding the government of the day to account. Kath did not trust the decision to send Fred and Tappy back to Spain, believing it was a decision to sentence them both to probable death for the cause and to eradicate a festering problem. Tappy, who was depressed by the whole affair, shared Kath's concern and Fred started to realize that politics was something more than political meetings. Maybe Kath and Tappy's concerns were justified.

Fred and Tappy went back to Harry Pollitt's office and told him straight about how they felt. After some considerable argument, Harry produced a letter assuring their authority while in Spain. The content of this extraordinary letter I was not able to trace during my four years researching this book. So many questions remain. Did the party leadership really think that Fred was dispensable? What was the real purpose of the letter? Did Fred and Kath really think that Fred could be shot in Spain by the Party if he fell out of line again? Why a letter, when he could so easily be killed on the frontline, like so many comrades before him? What is even more extraordinary is that Fred was almost certainly not a member of the Communist Party at this time, and this may be a reason why many communist historians have erased him from the period and communist history. Fred resigned from the Party following the incident when he knocked out a party official who had accused him of altering a receipt However, this meeting and Harry's visits to Spain suggest that, although Fred had resigned his membership, his high profile still made many think he was very much part of the Party leadership. Also, his going to Spain to fight the cause may have led the Party leadership to see this as a way for Fred to come back in, and that his walking out had just been like his knocking out of a party official – just a momentary lapse.

Against the wishes of Kath, Sandy, and his bride-to-be, Kitty, Fred set off for the Spanish frontline, this time with Tappy, crossing the Pyrenees on foot and wearing gym shoes to ensure they were as quiet as possible, as the French border guards were no friends of the Brigade.

On arrival at the battalion command, Fred was attached to the staff of the 15th Brigade. However, with events not much better than when he had left, Fred was again to become the battalion commander. The almost-open fighting between the anarchists and communists was affecting the leadership of the republican government and the Brigade itself. Meanwhile, the Americans and the British had their own squabble over power and control. Fred rose above the disorder, winning respect from all quarters. He convinced himself that the policy that best suited the interests of the Communist Party was the military success of the British battalion.

With Fred firmly in control of his battalion and with much improved discipline, Harry Pollitt arrived on one of his political visits on the eve of what would be known as the Teruel Offensive. Fred was suffering the worst bout of sickness he had had in the entire war. In London, doctors had told him that he probably needed an appendectomy, but Fred, always in a rush, thought it could wait another day. Now, just hours before a major offensive, he was too ill to move. He was taken to the Brigade hospital at Alcanaz. Kitty and Kath would be shocked to hear that the appendix had become gangrenous, and that a small piece of metal shrapnel had passed up his left leg from the knee, between the bone and the muscle, and entered the lining of the stomach. It was this that had caused the swelling of his leg, which he had thought had been an insect bite.

The action at Teruel was a success. Fred would be in bed for some time, although it did not stop him reading and writing his reports. The short-term gain, however, was lost in the counter-offensive, which, in part, would be responsible for ending the war. Sadly, Tappy was shot and killed, and it could so easily have been Fred. Following the battle, the Brigade demanded a court martial of two of the Brigade's men. Sentence was passed, and the two men were shot under the leadership of Sam, who had been Fred's deputy when he had been the Brigade's commanding officer. The firing squad were British volunteers. Fred wrote, '*Life seemed to stop. Somehow, too much had arrived at once, and I had reached the end of further physical effort.*'

Lying alone in a battlefield hospital bed, Fred began to experience a feeling of pleasant warmth. On lifting his hand out of the bed, he noticed it was covered in blood. Looking down, he saw he was lying in a bath of his own blood. No nursing volunteers were around, and Fred hurled what objects were within reach, and which his weak hands could grab, at the door to attract attention. With his feet and legs almost stone cold, Fred felt that it was inevitable that he was going to die and thought he should be writing a message to Kath and Kitty. He always kept their letters by his bed, together with a precious picture of a bunch of nasturtiums. Just as Fred was about to pass out, that thought of home made him call out for the last time, "Christ, help me!" Almost immediately, the door opened and in rushed a doctor from another part of the hospital who, by pure chance, was passing the door at that moment.

Thanks to the prompt action of the doctor and a team of Spanish medical students who pumped saline solution into Fred's battered body, his life was saved. The hemorrhage would return about once every five days and the pain it caused would stay with him his entire life. The poison from the appendix had eaten through the walls of the main artery, which could not be tied during the operation because he had been under anesthetic too long.

With the battle coming ever closer to the camp, Fred was taken to have his last words with his battalion before being taken to a better-equipped hospital in Barcelona, at Gandessa. However, upon his arrival, the battalion had already fled and his lads had moved on to defend the approach bridge across the Ebro, just north of Mora. Fred staggered out of the car that was taking him to Barcelona, unable to walk without holding the wound together with his hands, as he approached Sam to report for duty.

Sam, who was showing clear signs of exhaustion, told Fred, "You look as if you're going to die, but don't do it on me – I've got enough on my hands already." Fred realized he would be no use and continued his journey to Barcelona, where he discovered that talks were going on in Geneva for the withdrawal of the whole of the International Brigade, under the control of the League of Nations. The Ebro action would be their last fight, and Fred, defeated, would be going home – like a cat, he had his nine lives – to Kitty and Kath. Upon his return to England, he would also take time to visit the families of the men who never got home.

On Fred's arrival at Victoria Station, Kitty, Kath, and Sandy were on hand to welcome him and take him home, to 68 Ommaney Road. Mama had cooked up his favorite meal, and it certainly tasted much better than Spanish mule. Fred wondered how she found the time; the house was always a hive of activity often, in Fred's words, with 'a hundred and one people' visiting and staying at the house. Whilst Kath and Sandy led the campaigns, Mama ran the house as an efficient and welcoming hostess. Fred, still in great pain, could do little but hobble around the house and greet the throngs of visitors who dropped by.

Kitty and Kath, on top of everything else, were busy sorting out a home for Fred and Kitty to live in after their marriage, which was to take place on 21 May, 1938, at Lewisham Registry Office. Despite their differences with the Party, their wedding was an important affair and the Communist Party Leader, Harry Pollitt, would attend, along with other hugely important activists of the period such as Tom Mann, Charlotte Haldane, George House, Kath, Sandy, and Mama. Kitty's father was to give her away.

The reception was to be held at St. Pancras Town Hall, with some 1,100 guests in attendance, including many comrades from the battalion, as well as others from the many campaigns that had been fought on the streets of London.

The wedding was a wonderful event, although Fred was still not well. A friend, Bett Giles, whose husband would later become the president of the National Union of Teachers, slipped away quietly from the reception and got the fire going and Kitty and Fred's new home ready for the newlyweds. This was on Glenton Road, Lewisham. The kindness of the leaders of the unions, of the Communist and Labour Parties, of the Duncan household, and of local people ensured that the flat had everything a new couple starting out could need.

A couple of weeks after the wedding, the Communist Party asked Fred if he would organize and be responsible for the Dependents' Aid Committee, which, until this point, had been run by Charlotte Haldane. Whilst she had done a great job, within the rules and regulations of the Communist Party, it had been somewhat limited, and Fred was the one who could take it to the next level. Fred spent his time working with Labour leaders, like his friend Clement Attlee, and union leaders who had agreed to support the fund if an independent trust fund was set up with a board of trustees. As soon as Fred had established this fund, it raised £9,000, a huge sum at the time, from the Mine Workers' Union, the Amalgamated Engineering Union, and others.

Chapter Ten
The Last Queen of Scotland –
A Slow Train Home

The outbreak of World War II was not the only devastating news to hit the Duncan household. Sandy, after months of doctor and hospital visits, was diagnosed with mouth cancer. Kath, her 5-feet-2-inch frame riddled with tuberculosis and arthritis, was heartbroken. It did not just cause huge worry to her and Sandy, but also to Mama, who was in her 80s and still running the household like a tight ship while everything around them seemed to be crumbling. They had now moved, just around the corner, to Waller Road. Even when Sandy was unable to speak, he could still express his love for Kath by writing messages and smiley faces in the condensation which would build up overnight on their bedroom window.

The Duncan household at Ommaney Road had always been a home of love, laughter, and comradeship; very few other houses in London are as important to the struggles of the working class, and of what we would now call the LGBT movement, as 68 Ommaney Road. No other building had as many activists and political leaders of the age come through its doors and take tea and talk politics with Kath, Sandy, and Fred. Mama's great meals were forever bubbling away on the stove to feed the constant flow of people at the door who had come for legal and welfare advice, support with a rogue landlord, or help with employment issues. People would also drop by to help raise funds for doctors' and funeral bills or prison bail, or to debate the big issues of the day while they were hard at work making posters for the next big rally and protest. The state may have recorded the house as one full of revolutionaries and deviants, but to those who entered it, it was a place of wonder.

As Kath and Sandy were atheists, Christmas was the time they celebrated their wedding anniversary, except for the two when Kath was behind bars; and this fact ensured that Kath and Sandy would always be celebrating at this time of year with Mama, who was a devout Christian and for whom the Christian festival was hugely important. Nevertheless, the big celebration in the Duncan's household was always Burns Night. For one night only, the street would be full of the overspill of Scots and friends from across town who would arrive for her legendary Burns Night suppers, and people were always at a loss to understand how, even during the war years, Kath was always able to produce a Scotsman and his bagpipes. The return of a comrade from prison was also the occasion for a huge breakfast and a great welcome-home party.

For gay friends who in Kath's time were being jailed in as high numbers as those opposing fascism and the government's austerity agenda, a welcome home would take a different form: the gays in the house would help to dress all the men up as women in solidarity. That must have caused some concerns for the MI5 spies who watched the house's activities night and day. This was the house's way of saying 'Up yours!' as everything that went on at Ommaney Road would always be reported in minute detail back at the Home Office.

With both Sandy and Kath bed-ridden most days, the stream of visitors to their new home at 44 Waller Road was impressive and included all the big-name activists and politicians of the day, such as the Labour Party leader, Clement Attlee. While Attlee may have not been popular amongst the party leadership, he was much loved by the working poor and had carefully built up a strong friendship with Kath ever since he had been introduced to her by their mutual friend and fellow activist Fred Copeman during the Spanish Civil war campaign.

Kath had started to become increasingly disillusioned with the politics and politicking within the Communist Party, and especially with its position on World War II and its treatment of women, who felt the Party was failing them. Many women's sections were leaving, despite Kath's tour of the UK from Wales to Scotland to support them. Kath found it hard to square the circle, especially as her close friend, Fred Copeman, had left and joined Clement Attlee's Labour Movement. Mr. Attlee,

181

as she always addressed him, won her respect – and although she declined his invitation to stand as a Labour Party parliamentary candidate in the 1945 general election, on health grounds – she committed herself to spending every daylight hour she could rallying the comrades in Deptford to get the vote out for Labour.

Kath and Sandy were both unable to carry on the activism of the past. The days of Sandy helping Kath drop out of the rear window, with Mama holding his ankles, so that Kath could sneak out in Sandy's clothes and chalk up across town to publicize the next meeting, activist event, or slogan had long gone; although Kath's chalked messages and quick drawings to mobilize her community and her people had made her the Banksy of her time.

One report in the archive tells the story of a Frank N. Baker and a Mrs. C. F. Watt who, on a coach trip to celebrate May Day and carrying the Hammersmith Socialist Society banner – presently held at the Marx Memorial Library, in London – heard one of Kath's impassioned speeches on Deptford Broadway and wasted no time in re-joining the Party. They had both joined the Communist Party in the early years but had cancelled their membership under pressure from their union. That was what made Kath such an asset to the Communist Party; her powerful eloquence would always recruit new members and activists on a scale no one else could match.

19 Lind Street, St. Johns, Deptford. Kath Duncan's Home between 1945–1948

Kath had, however, taken on 'a young apprentice' in the person of 28-year-old Julius Cohen, who lived locally, on the Honor Oak Estate, Brockley. A chemist by trade, he was a Communist Party member and, like everyone else, thoroughly committed to the cause.

In May, 1940, though Kath had been able to secure some freedoms, the country was at war and communism and political activism had become extremely divisive issues. Local newspapers report that one Saturday night in Deptford, on the corner of Douglas Way and Amersham Vale, a communist chalk-writer figured in an angry scene in which the police intervened and Julius Cohen was arrested on the charge of using insulting words and behavior. Kath had never once been caught in all her 20 years of using her famous chalk, but her new apprentice was not so deft at escaping the clutches of the police. Cohen appeared in the dock at Greenwich Police Court on the following Monday and pleaded not guilty.

In the course of the proceedings against Cohen, Detective-Sergeant Smart said that he had seen the accused chalk on the roadway, '*Communist Meeting, Monday, 7.30pm. Who is your enemy?*' As he wrote the last sentence, one member of a crowd of several people who had gathered around replied, "You are the enemy." The accused had then exclaimed, "You mug! You don't know what you are fighting for." The crowd, which had become hostile, then moved towards him, and one person shouted, "You should be locked up. Let's set about him!" Cohen had a hurried conversation with two other men before walking away up Amersham Vale. When the witness, who was accompanied by Detective Du Rose, approached him, he took to his heels. They outpaced him, however, and told him he would be arrested for using insulting words and behavior calculated to cause a breach of the peace. Cohen remarked, "I have got to join your stinking army in a week or two." The witness told him he was very fortunate not to have met with some personal injury. He replied, "We communists have the courage of our own convictions." The officer added that Cohen had in his possession 44 copies of the *Daily Worker*, a telegram, a large lump of chalk, and a quantity of memoranda relating to communism. DS Smart reaffirmed that the crowd had become very hostile and were threatening the accused, and that this was the reason he had hurried away with his two friends – confederates, he presumed – pursued by the crowd.

In giving his version of these events, Cohen, speaking from the dock, said that, accompanied by two of his friends, he had chalked these slogans in three places; and that two or three people had stopped out of curiosity. He was not accustomed, he said, to shouting and bawling after he had done his chalking. He had left his two friends and walked away a little more hurriedly than usual because he had promised his wife he would be home by 10 pm. He did not know that the two persons who stopped him were police officers. When he had asked what was the matter, they had said, "You are going to rub that chalk out!" They used language to which he was not accustomed, and he objected to their demand. He denied that there was a hostile crowd or that he made any insulting comments about the army. "The army is not 'stinking'," he said. "It is composed of people like myself, but I am not going into the army in two weeks' time, as I am in a reserved occupation." He added that the witnesses confronted him in the street, not as police officers, but simply as persons irritated by what he had been writing.

Mr. John Eastwood, the magistrate, said that he was quite satisfied that what Cohen had said had indeed upset a certain number of people and that, if those remarks were what the witness described, he was not surprised at all. Cohen was fined 40 shillings. The police were still in complete control, and no word other than that of a police officer would be believed by any court. Just being a communist or a community activist, or just looking gay, was enough for police to arrest you. Kath had taken this risk, like so many others, day after day for the past ten years in Deptford.

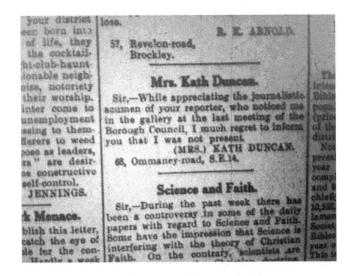

In 1940, Waller Road was hit by a bomb. Fred Copeman, on duty as a fire warden and aware that Sandy, Kath, and Mam were alone, rushed to their house at 44 Waller Road to find them all safe in the cellar of the house, which still stands today. It would be the last time he would see his best friend Sandy. It was on that same night that he wrote:

I knew that never again, whatever happened to me personally, could I support the Communist Party. Kath would not understand my decision and my attitude to Communist theory and practice, despite the callous indifference shown by the Party to Sandy and herself.

Sandy, with cancer of the tongue, was dying a slow and painful death. He left his home for the last time and was taken to Miller Hospital, Deptford. As word got out across the area, thousands of local residents lined the streets from the hospital and along Deptford Broadway, cheering as he passed, as if he were a war hero returning from battle. However, this was a battle he would not survive. Leaving his beloved Kath, Mama, and Deptford for his other home, Scotland, Sandy died in Glasgow on 24 March, 1941.

That Kath survived the war could be seen as a positive omen, and yet Kath's world was slowly drifting away from her. As 1945 arrived, she honored her pledge to rally the comrades of Deptford to secure a Labour election victory. It was hard for anyone with a modicum of human feeling to see how unwell Kath was and not admire and be moved by her tireless efforts to give every moment to the campaign. She was doing so much in the campaign office in Deptford to secure the keys to Number 10 for her friend Clement Attlee.

The Labour victory in 1945 and the epoch-making government that followed would address so many of the injustices Kath had devoted her life to combatting. The success was only tinged with sadness at the thought that Sandy was no longer alive to see the building of council homes and the creation of the National Health Service.

KATH DUNCAN'S RELEASE.

"RECEPTION" ARRANGED.

Mrs. Kath Duncan, the Greenwich and Deptford Communist leader, will be released from Holloway Gaol on Wednesday. A number of her women supporters will be at the gates when she leaves and they will escort her to Deptford, where "Kath" will address a meeting of the "comrades" in the Broadway

In the evening she will be welcomed back at a social gathering to be held at the Greenwich Baths Hall.

PLUMSTEAD DEATH AFTER ACCIDENT.

Harry George Shearman (72), of Bramblebury-road, Plumstead, who was knocked down by a pedal cyclist in Plumstead Common-road on December 31st, died in St. Nicholas Hospital on Wednesday.

Kath would cry a lot, not with the pain, but with joy at the fact that, after 60 years of struggle, the world, and her Deptford with it, was becoming a better place; and, in no small part, this was down to her and Sandy's activism. The world was a genuinely better place, in which the children that she had devoted so much of her life to would go on to have better life chances; and the promise that was made and broken – concerning World War I, that it would be the war to end all wars – would be kept this time and there would be no more war.

At some point between 1945 and 1948, Kath moved again to a new house, 19 Lind Street, Deptford. Whilst there is no paper record, 'Flip', a well-known character whose family goes back generations in Deptford, can still recall Kath living across the road from him. He remembers how smartly she was always turned out and the air of excitement generated merely by the mention of her name.

Much of what has been remembered and written about Kath has become blurred and inaccurate with time. Public records show that even communist and socialist historians, to whom Kath was of the greatest importance, made errors in what they wrote about her, such as stating that she was jailed only once.

Page 54

1954. DEATHS in the *District* of *Stracathro* in the *County* of *Angus*

In 1948, Kath and Mama were in such poor health that they moved to 30 Aberdare Gardens, in South Hampstead, probably because the rest of the household – Joan Ford, Leslie R. Gale, Nellie McWalters, Arthur Mills, Constance Olive, and Frederick T. Scott – were old comrades who felt they would look after them. The house still stands today, and at the time of writing, is up for sale at £5.6 million, or to rent at £13,400 per calendar month – breathtaking figures even today. In Kath's day, it was just several shillings a month.

Little is known of this period in Kath's history until 1951, when, at their home in Hampstead, Mama died of old age at 90, a staggeringly great age for the time. Mama would be the only family member who would die in London. She had refused to leave Kath alone to go back to Scotland, as Sandy had done, to her other daughter, Margaret, and her two grandchildren. She had been with Kath and accompanied her on her journey since she had given birth to her; dying would not change that.

After Mama's death, Kath returned to Deptford, to a new address, at 60 Chipley Street. Today, modern council housing stands where period houses used to stand.

Deptford Broadway in the 1930s

We owe a great to Kath Duncan. She could never have imagined that her civil rights protest on 30 July, 1934, which challenged the Metropolitan Police Act of 1839 – which authorized a police officer to arrest anyone for words or behavior which they thought could lead to a breach of the peace – would be so influential. This act was hugely popular with the police, who called it the 'Breathing Act' because a constable could interpret its general wording to arrest people for any kind of public nuisance, including breathing, looking gay, or giving a police officer a lashing with your tongue. In reality, this gave the police the power to ban any political meeting they saw fit.

In Kath Duncan's historic case, the National Council of Civil Liberties argued that Kath Duncan had not said a word, challenging the court's view, which stated that, on a past occasion, a disturbance had taken place after she had attended a rally for the unemployed. There was no evidence, however, that her speech or her actions had led to any disturbance. The 'logic' behind this seems to be that, if Kath Duncan's speech was to make the unemployed unhappy, the audience may, at a later date, commit a breach of the peace. The judgement by Lord Chief Justice Hewart was to make the police arbiters of freedom of speech and the right to public assembly. The case, setting a precedent in common law, was not dissimilar to that used in police states. It was hardly, if ever, used against Mosley's Blackshirts but was employed almost daily against those who were opposing government policy and challenging fascism.

Kath's case was heard at the King's Bench on 16 October, 1935, but as expected, it was lost. The following appeal to the House of Lords on 2 December, 1935, also failed. The high profile and sheer injustice of the trial, and the recognition it generated both for Kath Duncan and the National Council for Civil Liberties ensured that Westminster would eventually review the civil rights situation, although the police would resist in the short term.

Public unrest in 1999 would see the police rediscover the Duncan vs. Jones case and reactivate it. When a group of people were arrested for distributing flyers outside a furrier's and for protesting against animal cruelty and the fur trade, they were charged with obstructing the public highway. Citing the Duncan vs. Jones case, the defendants appealed and won their case. Other cases followed, including that of 21 people who had been arrested at Stonehenge for carrying banners bearing the words: '*Stonehenge Campaign – 10 years of Criminal Justice.*' In the same year, a coach-load of protestors on their way to the women's peace camp at Greenham Common was stopped on the motorway by the police and their driver was ordered to take the coach and all its passengers back to where it had come from, under threat of arrest. The final case, in 1999, in which the Duncan vs. Jones case invoked was the arrest of three peaceful, but vociferous, preachers after some members of a crowd that had gathered around them seemed about to become threatening and hostile. In this case, the presiding judge ruled that freedom of speech meant nothing unless it included the freedom to be irritating and contentious. At last, by the end of 1999, the judgment against Kath Duncan could no longer be used to suppress civil liberties.

Kath's last days were probably spent reflecting on the people she had welcomed into her home and into her heart. Fred Copeman was awarded the OBE for services to London during the Second World War. A leader of the biggest mutiny in British military history being welcomed by the King with such an honor! You can imagine the smile this must have put on Kath's face. Her boy, her mutineer, honored thus by the state he had so bravely challenged to do better for its citizens. Fred went on to become a much-loved and dedicated Labour councilor on Lewisham Council, married to his beloved Kitty, with whom he had two children.

In the 1930s, Deptford quickly and successfully saw off the Greenshirts, a new political movement that had been established in the area to counter the popularity of Kath's Communist Party.

In 2008, a new political party would take on Lewisham Council and the wider state with radical activism and a popular socialist agenda very much in the line of Kath Duncan. This was Lewisham People Before Profit, an alliance of the Socialist Party, Greens, Old Labour, Lib. Dems, and even some Tories. Its candidates won 20,000 votes in the local council elections, coming second to Labour in six wards. In Deptford, they came second, with 26% of the vote. While in the Telegraph Hill ward – the area in which Kath had lived from the 1930s until 1945 and which had become one of the most radical council wards in the UK, consistently returning and electing to office socialist councilors such as Ian Page and Chris Flood – two young men in the mold of Kath also backed Lewisham People Before Profit's candidate, with 35% of the vote.

Today, People Before Profit is a global group with elected members in the Irish Parliament, in Stormont, and in local councils on both sides of the border. Kath would be delighted that, in 2018, a socialist like Jeremy Corbyn would once again be leading a genuinely socialist Labour Party along the lines she endorsed and fought for with her friend Clement Attlee.

In January, 1954, Kath's sister arrived at 60 Chipley Street, Deptford, which, like the first house in Hackney where Kath lived, no longer stands; although, new council housing has since been built on the site. She had come to take her sister home, for Kath, just like Sandy, wanted to die in Scotland.

As she was extremely sick, an ambulance was booked to take her to Euston station. As the ambulance driver was helping to carry Kath into the back of the ambulance, he caught a glimpse of her hair, still flame red, and her sparkling blue eyes and realized that this was Kath Duncan. "Poor Kath!" he said. "But you weren't always like this. I will always remember you as last I saw you." And he gave her a kiss.

Kath passed away on 14 August, 1954, at Stracathro Hospital, Brechin. It had been almost 10 years since Kath had climbed out of her sick bed to mobilize the comrades to get the vote out for Labour, and 20 years since her activism had made her the most famous political activist of her age.

I am sure Kath would approve of how she came to my attention, and of the good effects her story continues to have.

As I was seeking out new ways to fund the We Care Food Bank that Barbara Raymond and I had set up on New Cross Road, in Deptford, we organized the Deptford Heritage Festival. As part of this, we wrote and produced a radical history book of Deptford which included a local history walk. It was while I was working on the book and the festival that I came across the life of Kath and Sandy Duncan. The sale of this book, which contains my first summary of Kath's story, and my other book, *Food Bank Britain*, continue to fund my We Care projects across the UK. And I am sure that Kath would

191

approve, despite her undoubted dismay at the political and social tragedy that renders such projects necessary.

In 2015, while researching Kath's life in greater depth, I came across another fascinating working-class story in Deptford. This was the tale of the 500 Deptford ship builders and craftsmen who left with Peter the Great in the 1800s to build the first Russian navy. My research attracted the interest of the Russian government, who instructed its heritage committee to investigate what had become of the Deptford 500. For my work in bringing together histories and heritages of Deptford and Russia, I was presented with a medal from the Russian people by the Russian Ambassador in London. As Kath was a lover and friend of Russia, I felt that this medal was in part for her.

Ever since the success of the first Deptford Heritage Festival, the Russian embassy holds a 'Peter the Great' day in Deptford every May. And in 2017, it raised the money to restore a carved stone in Sayers Court Park, Deptford, below the mulberry tree that is supposed to have been planted by Peter the Great. Kath would be proud that Deptford still celebrates today its links to the Russian people, despite the political difficulties. She would also be gratified that the woman who so loved dramatics would have a play, *Liberty*, written about her, which is set to be performed in China in 2018 and in the USA in February 2019, where the Harvey Milk Institute in San Francisco wants this play about Kath's life and struggle for civil rights to be staged as a key event in the LGBT History Month. The theme of this event is history, activism, and people; the Red Blouses would be delighted.

Other plays about Kath's life and activism have been written in the past, but I was unable to find any copies while doing the research for this book. I would be grateful to hear from any reader who may have more information about this. Similarly, I was only able to find the very few pictures of Kath Duncan that have appeared in this, and I could find none of Sandy, so I would again be very grateful to hear from anyone who has or knows of others, or indeed has any additional information about Kath of any kind.

What an amazing life! Is it really too much to ask that the schools that have taught us so much about our kings and queens now start to teach our children something about our amazing working-class heroes, especially the women who, at huge personal cost, have fought and won our battles to secure the freedoms we enjoy today? Is it wrong to ask you to lobby the relevant bodies in Hackney, Camden, Lewisham, Kirkcaldy, and the Scottish Parliament to give Kath a blue plaque, at the very least? Should not my play about Kath and her actions that led to formation of the National Council of Civil Liberties not be on every drama group's 'must-do' play list?

In every town, a Kath Duncan will always be found, moving amongst those most in need, always putting the interests of others before their own, while always praying that poverty and inequality will become something of a bygone age. Should we not value and celebrate their lives too?

Word was quick to circulate in Deptford that Kath had gone. Thousands turned out on Deptford Broadway, and many a speech and story were told; and then, as they decided to make a toast, a silence. How do we remember our comrade who did so much for every man, woman, and child here today? Let us make a toast. "She was our queen," a voice yelled out. Yes, that's the toast: 'To the Last Queen of Scotland'. This is how Deptford said goodbye to her and how it would remember her, in the full vigor of her radiant personality, leading the people in the long march towards a socialist Britain, for which she gave her life.

In 1957, a young black woman would arrive in Deptford from the West Indies. She would tirelessly champion the poor, campaign on housing and against social injustice in all its forms, march for equality, be the first black woman to lead a political party, and be a co-founder of the country's largest food bank – We Care. Today, at 80 years young, she continues her work amongst the poor in Deptford. The name of this other working-class hero: Barbara Raymond.

Barbara Raymond – no end to her activism

CPSIA information can be obtained
at www.ICGtesting.com
Printed in the USA
BVHW042244260319
543830BV00007B/39/P